Handbook of
Every Day Islam

Answers to the Most Commonly Asked Questions
Concerning the Faith of Islam and its Followers

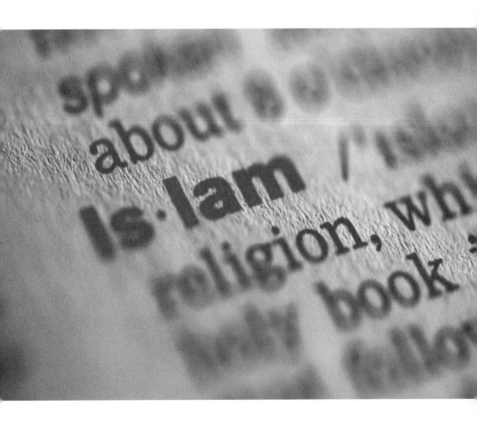

Imam Hassan Qazwini

Compiled by Dr. Joffer Hakim

ISBN: 978-0-9910250-0-8

Library of Congress Control Number: 2013920800

© Copyright 2013 by Islamic Center of America

Published by
Islamic Center of America
19500 Ford Road
Dearborn, MI 48128
www.icofa.com · admin@icofa.com
313.593.0000

Layout and Cover Design by
Islamic Publishing House
Kitchener, ON
www.iph.ca

Printed in Canada by *Marquis*

Contents

In the Name of God, the Most Gracious, the Most Merciful

Preface

Islam, the third monotheistic religion after Judaism and Christianity, has much in common with these two faiths, and yet it is also the most comprehensive. For Muslim scholars, Islam is not only a religion but also a way of life, and it also completed the mission of earlier prophets. As the last divine message, Islam offers a solution for every challenge we face.

Muslims are encouraged to be inquisitive. In the Islamic tradition, we leave the door for seeking knowledge wide open. Only by searching ourselves, our world, and our spiritual beliefs logically and rationally can we truly embrace our faith. Thus, the Prophet of Islam, Muhammad (ṣ) said: "Seeking knowledge is obligatory upon every Muslim male and female."

Islam removes all psychological barriers and asks Muslims to educate themselves about their faith. Knowledge, then, is the primary measuring stick for how we should regard individuals.

About This Book

This book is a product of the tremendous volume of inquiries about Islam I have received over the years and covers most aspects of Islamic doctrine. E-mail and the Internet have made knowledge so much more accessible and have correspondingly increased the number of questions I receive from Muslims and non-Muslims alike.

More than ever, Muslims are recommitting themselves to explorations of the faith, and non-Muslims wish to understand the principles of Islam. The most practical way for me to aid their quests was to share the answers I have written to my correspondents' most common and urgent questions.

Their names, of course, have been removed, but the issues they struggle with are universal. The answers have been refined and in some cases expanded for the sake of publication. My hope is that a wider audience will adopt them as a tool to improve its understanding of Islam.

Acknowledgments

I express my deepest appreciation and gratitude to four individuals who were helpful in assembling this book:

1. My friend Dr. Joffer Hakim, an anesthesiologist who spent countless hours compiling, reviewing, and categorizing the questions for publication. Dr. Hakim is a dear friend who forsook much-needed rest and relaxation to finish this project. He has been so enthusiastic, dedicated, and persistent. Many thanks to him.

2. My son, Sayed Muhammad Baqer, who also spent many hours reviewing/editing the manuscript and tracing the correct Islamic references, including Qur'anic verses and the original sources of ahadith. He is currently studying at the Islamic Seminary of Qom in Iran. May God illuminate his path.

3. My friend Brad Crawford, who edited the book. Brad also helped me with writing my first English book, *American Crescent: A Muslim Cleric on the Power of His Faith, the Struggle against Prejudice, and the Future of Islam and America.* God bless him.

4. Sister Arifa Hudda, who also contributed to reading the entire manuscript, made timely suggestions while reviewing the book and was instrumental in the editing of the text. May God reward her.

5. Shaykh Saleem Bhimji, from the Islamic Publishing House, who designed the cover page and typeset the book.

Note on Expressions

In Islam, the blessed names of the Holy Prophet Muhammad, the infallible Imams of Ahlulbayt, and all Prophets of God are to be treated with utmost respect, as respecting these important individuals is respecting God. It is highly recommended to praise them and to pray for them after mentioning their name or referring to them. For the sake of continuity, we have abbreviated the following expressions in this book after mentioning their names.

The expression "(ṣ)" is used after the name of Prophet Muhammad (ṣ). It is short for the Arabic phrase *"sallallahu alayi wa alihi wa sallam,"* which means "May God send His prayers on him and his family."

The expression (a) is used after mentioning the Prophets of God, the name of the twelve Imams of Ahlulbayt, Lady Fatima al-Zahra, and other noble members of the Ahlulbayt. It is short for the Arabic phrase *"alayhi salam,"* which mean "peace be upon him," or the phrase *"alayha salam,"* which means "peace be upon her."

Introduction to Islam

1. What makes Islam different from Judaism and Christianity?

The three monotheistic religions - Judaism, Christianity and Islam - trace their roots to one tree: the Abrahamic faith. The faith of the patriarch, Prophet Abraham (a), essentially stands on the belief of one Omnipotent, Omniscient God and the belief in a Day of Judgment. Therefore, these three monotheistic religions share an array of teachings that extend from basic moral values such as being kind to others, offering good deeds, repelling injustice and wrongdoing, regarding human life with sanctity, all the way to many day to day moral imperatives that an individual meets in his or her personal and public life. In the Judeo-Christian belief system, these moral standards are manifested in the Ten Commandments, while in Islam they cover a wider range of moral standards and values on a daily basis.

Islam stands out among the three monotheistic faiths by embracing a more comprehensive and elaborate path that is not limited to a particular moral commandment, but extends to all aspects of socioeconomic and political life. As the third and last monotheistic religion, Muslims believe that Islam established the precepts of a universal religion that is aimed at nourishing the spiritual needs of all of humanity. In comparison to Judaism and Christianity, Islam added newer and broader dimensions to people's spiritual, social, and family life. Far from being abstract, these dimensions are vigorous and extremely relevant to the growth of humankind's spiritual life. Islam not only contributed to the growth of our spiritual lives, but it also plays a great role in our secular lives as well. For instance, Islam brought forth a comprehensive social justice system in which the poor and the wealthy, the powerful and the weak, and people from all races must live in a harmonious community that is based on justice, equality and fairness. Islam also offers a political theory based on the concept of *shura*, or consultation, that lays out the foundations for governance and people's inclusion based on Islamic moral principles.

Moreover, Islam offers an elaborate judiciary system that regulates punitive codes based on divinely inspired teachings. Many Muslim scholars also believe that Islam embraces an economic system that limits the growing selfish tendencies of the capitalist system, yet recognizes personal ownership and entrepreneurship. Islam also rejects the communist and socialist systems that strip people from their Godly given freedoms.

Islam further stands out for its remarkable emphasis on respect for one's parents to the extent that the holy Qur'an couples worshipping God with doing good to one's parents.[1] While going to mass on Sunday defines many Christians as being observant, it is not enough for observant Muslims to go to mosque only once or twice a week. Muslims are required to pray five times a day, whether they are at home, at work, or on vacation. Furthermore, while one's actions for many Christians are secondary to believing in Jesus as the redeemer of one's sins, Islam places great emphasis on one's own actions. The holy Qur'an recognizes "the believers" as only those who believe *and* do good deeds. Unlike modern

---

[1] *Noble Qur'an*, Suratul Naml (27), verse 23

Judaism, Islam recognizes no boundaries and is open for everyone. Furthermore, whereas many Jews today do not believe in the Day of Judgment, this belief is an integral part of the Islamic belief system. While Islam recognizes both Judaism and Christianity, and one cannot be a Muslim without believing in Prophets Moses (a) and Jesus (a), Christianity and Judaism do not recognize Islam. Therefore, in this regard, Islam is more inclusive.

Muslims believe that the Arabic Qur'an we have today is the actual word of God. Prophet Muhammad (ṣ) conveyed it exactly how it was revealed to him by God, without paraphrasing any part of it. Furthermore, the Qur'an has remained unchanged throughout the centuries and the text that we have today is the exact text that existed during the time of Prophet Muhammad (ṣ). To the contrary, many Christians believe that the Bible is a paraphrase or an encapsulation of the teachings of Jesus, and not his words verbatim. Jews believe that the Torah is a divinely inspired historic book, and not necessarily the exact words of God. However, despite the differences between Islam and the other monotheistic religions, there remain certain similarities and common ground, and the Qur'an instructs us to build bridges based on this mutual ground.[2]

2. What do Muslims believe?

Islam is based on a set of beliefs and practices. The most important belief, which serves as Islam's foundation, is the belief in one God. Islam strictly rejects polytheism and atheism. The second most important belief is accepting Prophet Muhammad (ṣ) as the final of

---

[2] *Noble Qur'an*, Surat Aale Imran (3), verse 64

the 124,000 messengers of God. Therefore, every Muslim believes in these two declarations of faith, which are commonly known as the shahada (testifying to the Oneness of God and the Prophethood of Prophet Muhammad (ṣ). Muslims also believe in God's complete justice and mercy, and they believe in the Day of Judgment, which is when all of humanity will be resurrected and judged before God.

While these beliefs serve as the core of Islam, one's faith is not complete without the practices that God has mandated for us to perform. Important Islamic practices (or rituals) include praying five times a day, fasting for thirty days during the month of Ramadhan, giving charity to the poor and deprived, making the pilgrimage to Mecca at least once in a lifetime, striving in the way of God, resisting one's evil temptations and desires, encouraging what is good, and discouraging what is evil. Muslims believe that this life is a trial for us, and thus we will experience difficulties and hardships to varying degrees according to our abilities. Islam encourages every Muslim to pursue knowledge from the cradle to the grave, and Muslim scholars believe that science is a necessary pursuit in this life. The greatest and most noble cause is to work for justice, and there is no honor greater than helping and serving other people. We also believe that in this life we must strive to achieve a high level of spirituality and protect ourselves from drowning in materialism.

3. Why is Prophet Muhammad (s) so important in Islam?

Today, around 1.5 billion Muslims consider themselves to be the followers of Prophet Muhammad (ṣ). His name is the most common name in the world today. Prophet Muhammad (ṣ) was born in the year 570 A.D. in the holy city of Mecca. For the first forty years of his life, he had developed an unparalleled reputation of being the most trustworthy and truthful man in Mecca; then at the age of forty, God revealed the Qur'an to him and instructed him to spread the religion of Islam. Although Prophet Muhammad (ṣ) is the last prophet and messenger of God, he is the most outstanding of God's 124,000 messengers. His words are binding commandments for all Muslims, who also believe that he was infallible—meaning error free and protected from any vice, wrongdoing or sin.

He never spoke from his own desire, but everything that he said and did was an instruction from God. The Qur'an states:

Your companion does not err, nor does he go astray; Nor does he speak out of desire. It is not but revelation that is revealed (to him)[3].

The Qur'an also teaches us that the Prophet has more authority over us than even our own parents or anyone else:

The Prophet has a greater claim on the faithful than they have on themselves.[4]

An important aspect that distinguished Prophet Muhammad (ṣ) from many of the other prophets is that while most other prophets were private citizens during their lives, Prophet Muhammad (ṣ) was a community leader, statesman, and an active contributor to social, economic and political life. Keeping this in mind sheds light

---

[3] *Noble Qur'an*, Suratul Najm (53) verses 2-4
[4] *Noble Qur'an*, Suratul Ahzab (33), verse 6

on his life and the challenges that he faced. Some westerners compare Prophet Muhammad (ṣ) to Prophet Jesus (a) and claim that Muhammad (ṣ) was a violent man because he engaged in many battles while Jesus (a) never did. Prophet Jesus (a) was not a statesman, and hence he was not in a position to engage in battle. When Prophet Muhammad (ṣ) established the first Muslim community in Medina, he was attacked by many of his surrounding enemies, especially the pagans of Mecca. All of the eighty-two or so battles in which he participated were defensive ones and were aimed at protecting Islam and the Muslim community from outside forces.

Throughout history, Prophet Muhammad (ṣ) has been considered by many historians and intellectuals to be the most influential man in human history. He was, as Michael Hart put it, the most successful figure in history at the religious and secular levels. Not only was he able to change the face of the Arabian Peninsula, but he also succeeded in changing human history and making Islam the dominant force worldwide only fifty years after his death. Islam spread to many territories stretching all the way from the Atlantic Ocean in Morocco to the borders of China. Today, there are more than 1.5 billion people (about one-fifth of the world's population) who regard Prophet Muhammad (ṣ) as their role model and consider themselves to be his followers. Many great non-Muslim thinkers and authors have passionately written about Prophet Muhammad (ṣ). Recently, Karen Armstrong, an author, commentator and a former Catholic religious sister; Leslie Hazleton, a Jewish writer; and John Esposito, a professor at

Georgetown University, have all written books about Prophet Muhammad.

4. Why is the Arabic language so important in Islam?

Arabic is the language of the Qur'an, which is the actual word of God. It is also the language which was spoken by Prophet Muhammad and his revered successors. In order to grasp a full understanding of Islam, which is based on the Qur'an and the *hadith,* one must be well versed in the Arabic language. Ordinary Muslims are not required to be fluent or experts in Arabic in order to practice their faith and establish a connection with God. Their need for learning Arabic stands at a minimum, such as the Opening Chapter of the Qur'an, another short chapter from the Qur'an, and a few phrases praising God that are to be recited in the five daily prayers.

For those people who seek a deeper understanding of Islam or aim at becoming experts, however, mastering Arabic becomes extremely essential; and this is why all orientalists and non-Muslim experts on Islam have had to learn Arabic fluently. It is worth mentioning that only 18% percent of the global Muslim population, which is about 1.5 billion, is Arab. The vast majority of Muslims do not speak Arabic and their knowledge of the Arabic language is quite limited.

5. If Islam is the religion of true believers, then why did it not come first?

Muslim theologians embrace the idea that the spiritual growth of humanity took the same course that an individual takes in his or her own intellectual growth. Our intellectual journey begins as soon as we are born, and we transition from complete ignorance to accumulating knowledge about ourselves and the world that surrounds us. Our parents take us to kindergarten, which serves as our first academic institution where we receive formal education. Then we continue our intellectual journey to elementary school, and as our comprehension and intellectual capacity advances, we excel to higher education and go on to high school. As adults, we pursue our intellectual journey by attending college or university, where we specialize in certain fields and establish our lifetime careers and professions. Upon graduating from these higher studies, we become concerned with establishing a marital and family life, and we continue our life journey. An indispensable aspect of our life journey is how it is gradual. One cannot advance and develop his or her intellectual capacity without gaining knowledge and experience gradually, or step by step. This enables us to gauge ourselves by examining our current state, the state that is above us, and the state that is beneath us.

Just like an individual advances in life through multiple phases and stages, in order for humanity to expand its spiritual growth, it is also required to go through various spiritual phases as well. Prophet Abraham (a) laid the first, universal foundation for monotheism. Then, Judaism came to form the first layer of a formal organized religion. As humankind advanced towards spirituality, Christianity formed the second layer. As humanity further progressed and achieved greater preparation for God's last word, Islam came to form the last and final layer. If we employ contemporary terms, we can say that Islam represents the stage of going to college or university. However, we must remember that one cannot jump to college without going through the first and second stages of one's academic pursuit, which are elementary school and high school. Similarly, humanity could not have jumped to embracing God's final message without receiving the earlier religions. Therefore, Islam is in essence a continuation of the previous monotheistic religions that were revealed by God.

6.   What is the significance of Mecca to Muslims?

As God tells us in the holy Qur'an[5], Mecca embraced the first house of worship which was built by God's command. According to our narrations, the first person to build this house was Prophet Adam. Later, God instructed Prophet Abraham (a) and his son Prophet Ishmael (a) to rebuild the house in the form of a cubic shaped building known as the Ka'bah. The Ka'bah today sits in the middle of the Grand Mosque in Mecca. Upon completing the construction of the Ka'aba, God commanded Abraham to stand on a nearby mountaintop to call upon and invite all people to perform the pilgrimage to Mecca. Since that day, the tradition of pilgrimage to Mecca started, and for centuries many Arabs even in the pre-Islamic era used to perform the pilgrimage to Mecca. After the advent of Islam, however, the pilgrimage to Mecca became a universal phenomenon that today attracts over 15 million pilgrims every year, of which three million visit during the Hajj season. The pilgrims come from almost every country around the world.

Additionally, Mecca is deemed as the center of the Muslim prayer, and all Muslims must direct themselves to the Ka'bah

---

[5] *Noble Qur'an*, Surat Aale Imran (3), verse 96

wherever they are once they want to pray. Therefore, millions of Muslims pray to the direction of Mecca daily from all of the world continents. Lastly, Mecca is the birthplace of Prophet Muhammad. It was his hometown, as he lived there for fifty-three years, of which thirteen years were after his appointment to Prophethood.

7. Is Islam a Peaceful Religion?

Islam is undoubtedly a peaceful religion. Whenever Muslims greet one another, the first words that they exchange are "*As-salaamu alaikum*" ("Peace be with you") and "*Wa alaykum as-salaam*" ("And with you, be peace"). Indeed, one of the ninety-nine names of God in Islam is "*As-Salaam*" - "The Peace." The Qur'an says:

> *Whoever slays a soul, unless it be for manslaughter or for mischief in the land [genocide], it is as though he slew all of mankind; and whoever keeps it alive, it is as though he kept alive all of mankind.*[6]

In another passage the Qur'an states:

> *God does not forbid you respecting (meaning He compels us to respect) those who have not made war against you on account of [your] religion, and have not driven you forth from your homes, that you show them kindness and deal with them justly; surely God loves the doers of justice.*[7]

But the best proof of Islam's peaceful message is Prophet Muhammad (ṣ) himself. He fought many battles in his life, all of which were defensive and aimed at protecting his people and

---

[6] *Noble Qur'an*, Suratul Ma'idah (5), verse 32

[7] *Noble Qur'an*, Suratul Mumtahina (60), verse 8

community. He established an elaborate framework for just war in Islam. Prophet Muhammad (ṣ) received God's message in seventh-century Arabia, at a time of frequent warfare, instability, and for many, deprivation. Tribes routinely raided neighboring tribes to obtain life's necessities, while ignoring society's underprivileged and enslaved. One reason Prophet Muhammad (ṣ) met with such violent resistance in Mecca upon the revelation of Islam was his advocacy of a new social order. He stressed people's essential quality, called on the rich to help take care of the poor, and preached that violence should be avoided wherever possible. He condemned female infanticide; and he purchased slaves and would then set them free. As he developed the means, he adopted many orphaned children and raised them in his household. Many of the earliest converts to Islam were from the underclass.

Critics of Islam cite other passages from the Qur'an to justify their claim of Islam being a violent religion. Those verses that seem to condone aggression or warfare are taken out of context and are less shocking than line-by-line quotes from other holy books, such as the Bible. In Islam's early years, Muslims were a small band of vulnerable and controversial followers who were engulfed by brutal adversaries. The real threat those adversaries posed, whether in Mecca or Medina, required Prophet Muhammad (ṣ) to set the boundaries of defense without expanding war. Numerous passages in the Qur'an make this clear, and the rule is summarized in chapter 8, verse 61:

If the enemies incline towards peace, then you also incline towards peace, and trust in God, for He is the One who hears and knows all things.

Other examples in the Qur'an include chapter 2, verse 190, chapter 2, verse 194, and chapter 4, verse 90. Perhaps the single act of Prophet Muhammad that mostly demonstrates Islam's rejection of violence and push for peace is when he returned triumphant to Mecca. Mecca harbored many criminals who had blood on their hands; and the Meccans had waged tens of battles against the Prophet and the Muslims. They even conspired with many tribes and groups to uproot Islam, and they imposed various sanctions on Muslims to the point that some of them starved to death. They tortured many Muslims and murdered others. Yet, when Prophet Muhammad (ṣ) entered Mecca in the year 630 A.D., he accepted the surrender of its inhabitants and granted them all complete amnesty. Some of the Muslims demanded that the Meccans be punished for their crimes, but Prophet Muhammad (ṣ) refused to show them anything but mercy. Many, in awe of his mercy and kindness, converted to Islam.

Another example of Islam's tolerance and justice is Imam Ali (a). *The Peak of Eloquence,* a collection of his letters and sayings, relates a story of the Islamic attitude toward freedom and justice. During the period of Imam Ali's (a) caliphate in Kufa, Iraq, a bold non-Muslim man took Imam Ali's (a) shield and claimed it as his own. The witnesses who could have refuted the man's claim were traveling, yet Imam Ali (a) asked a judge to hear the case and render a decision. In the course of the hearing, the judge honored Imam Ali (a) and tried to address him as "Commander of the Believers," but Imam Ali (a) insisted on absolute neutrality in the case, and he lost the dispute—and his shield—because of it. Afterward, the man caught up with Imam Ali (a) and returned the shield. "Imam, teach me Islam," he said. "I am Jewish, but I want to convert."

"Did anybody force you to do that?" Imam Ali (a) asked.

"No, Imam," he said, "but your behavior of treating even a non-Muslim subject as your equal, the prestige you granted to justice and fair play...made me feel that Islam is a great religion. You could have easily ordered me to be killed and my property confiscated, and nobody would have dared to ask reasons for your actions...I have never heard of such a ruler like this before you."

Islam's peaceful nature, however, has been manipulated historically by schemers and extremists. There are no membership requirements to be a Muslim - one must only profess faith and perform the obligatory duties, such as prayers, charity, and fasting. Today, we still have violent extremists who exploit Islam as a religious rationale for their acts, but they cannot and should not speak for Islam. The Islam that Prophet Muhammad (ṣ) advocated is peaceful and has no room for violence, terrorism or extremism.

8. What is Sharia and do all Muslims follow it?

Sharia, simply put, is a code of conduct or a set of laws and rulings; and therefore, technically every religion has a Sharia. The Ten Commandments, for example, are part of the Judeo-Christian Sharia. The Qur'an states:

> To each among you We have appointed a law and a way, and if God had pleased He would have made you (all) a single people, but that He might try you in what He gave you, therefore strive with one

another to hasten to virtuous deeds; to God is your return, all of you.[8]

Since Islamic law has a very broad spectrum, Sharia may refer to the entire body of Islamic law or it may refer to a particular aspect of Islamic law. Therefore, the word may be used to refer to the Islamic dietary system, Islamic laws pertaining to prayer and fasting, the Islamic political, economic and judiciary systems, or the punitive code. One must exercise caution when using the word Sharia as to what aspect of the Islamic law is being referred to.

When the word Sharia is mentioned by Muslims in the United States, it generally refers to the compliance of Muslims to the day to day Islamic laws that generally apply to them as individuals, such as eating halal food, marital relations, observing the *hijab* (head covering), or abiding by the Islamic banking system which prohibits usury. Establishing an Islamic government or theocracy, as the media often suggests, is not referred to when American Muslims speak of Sharia. The understanding of Sharia law in the U.S. could be paralleled to the Jewish law that requires observant Jews to eat Kosher, and other laws that pertain to their everyday lives within the context of living under American law, such as the laws of segregation in the synagogue, or the prohibition of shaking hands with the opposite gender. Hence, Sharia is basically a process that helps Muslims integrate into bigger society while maintaining their religious identity.

Many Islamophobes today, with the help of the media, invoke fear in American society and question the loyalty of Muslim

---

[8] *Noble Qur'an*, Suratul Ma'idah (5), verse 48

Americans by offering their own interpretation of what Sharia law is. They constantly wave the card of Sharia law without understanding what it is. They do so in order to gain political support and momentum, thereby serving their own personal interests and agendas. Many politicians and policy makers who have vehemently advocated for anti-Sharia legislation do not have the slightest clue about what Islamic Sharia is.[9] They equate Sharia with violence and terrorism, often by invoking an image of the infamous Taliban stoning women. Sharia is aimed at providing a framework for Muslims to integrate into the larger society - it is not aimed at creating conflict with the larger society.

---

[9] For example, Alabama Republican State Senator Allen Gerald, who pushed for anti-Sharia legislation, gave this answer when he was asked about what Sharia law is: "I don't have my file in front of me. I wish I could answer you better." Source: http://onfaith.washingtonpost.com/onfaith/undergod/2011/03/anti-shariah_laws_legislating_religiosity.html

The Big Picture

9.   Who is God in Islam?

Muslims believe in the same God of Abraham (a), Moses (a) and
Jesus (a). God is One, Omnipotent, Omnipresent, Omniscient, and
Self-Sufficient. In the Arabic language, God is referred to with the
word Allah. Some non-Muslims have the wrong notion that Allah
is the God in Islam only, and He is a different deity than the one in
Judaism and Christianity. However, just like God is Yahweh in
Hebrew and Khoda in Persian, He is Allah in Arabic. Arabic
speaking Christians also call Him Allah.

Islam teaches us that God has two kinds of attributes. The first
are the "attributes of beauty," and these are the attributes that
God possesses, such as being alive, the sustainer, the creator, the
powerful, the giver, and so on. The second are the "attributes of
glory," and these are the attributes that are negated from God,
such as having a partner, begetting a son, being begotten, being
weak, being in need, and so on. God is not corporeal, as He has no
physical body. Had God been a physical entity, He would have been
limited and in need of space, shape and matter, but God is above
all of these limitations. To put these two types of attributes in
simple terms, the attributes of beauty are those that God is or has,
and the attributes of glory are those which God is not or does not
have.

In English and many other languages, the word Allah is a
masculine word, so He is referred to by the masculine pronoun He.

This however, does not suggest in any way that God is male. God has no gender, and to believe that He is male amounts to blasphemy. The masculine pronoun that is used for Him is strictly linguistic, and it has no implications beyond that whatsoever.

God refers to Himself in the holy Qur'an with the plural pronoun "we." This might confuse some, especially some Christians whose mind is embedded with the trinity. This pronoun is called the "majestic we," and God uses it to glorify Himself and evoke His majesty and power. Many kings, for instance, refer to themselves with this word to indicate their glory and power.

10. How do we know that there is only one God for all of humanity?

The beauty of God's oneness, a theological concept we know as monotheism, is that it takes no special knowledge or even belief in any particular religion or doctrine to prove. The fine-tuned order of the natural world all around us speaks of one Creator. All we need to do is ponder over His creation. Earth and sky, fire and water, plant and animal all work together, and a change in even one small element affects all of those around it, and all of this reveals a single Creator who perfectly designed everything. If there was more than one God, our entire universe would be chaotic and inscrutable because multiple gods could never agree on everything. Their divergent laws and systems would inevitably clash and undermine, rather than reinforce, life's complexities. The Noble Qur'an explains this in the following passage:

> If there had been in them any gods except [the one true] God, they would have certainly been in a state of disorder; therefore glory be

to God, the Lord of the dominion, above what they attribute (to Him). [10]

By definition, God is All-Knowing, All-Powerful, and Eternal; and if He was anything otherwise, then the creation of the universe would not have been as it is. Thus, if there was more than one god, each would have had limited powers and therefore by definition, *not* be God.

Imagine if one god willed to do something, the other gods could either prevent or could not prevent the first one. If they could, the first one becomes limited, and if they could not, then they would be limited!

For Muslims, the oneness of God is essential because we strive to abide by God's law and fulfill His will for us—an impossible task if there are multiple gods with conflicting standards and expectations. (One name for Islam, *Deen al-Tawhid,* even means "The religion of One God.")

Imam Ali (a), the cousin, son-in-law and successor of Prophet Muhammad (ṣ) once said to his son Imam al-Hasan (a): "Remember, my son, had there been any other god besides the One, he would have also sent his own messengers and prophets, and they would have pointed out to humankind the domain and glory of this second god, and you would have also seen them. But no such incident ever took place. He is One God whom we should all recognize and worship." [11]

---

[10] *Noble Qur'an,* Suratul Anbiya (21), verse 22
[11] *Nahj al-Balagha (Peak of Eloquence),* vol. 3, p. 44, letter no. 31

11. Why is there evil in this world?

Scholars have two views regarding the presence of evil in this world. The first group of scholars believes that everything God has created is good, and He did not create any evil. Evil basically means an absence of goodness. Thus, by this definition, evil is not created by God - humans or human ignorance, greed and cruelty have created it.

When a murderer takes a knife and kills an innocent person, what part of this process is evil? Is it the knife? The knife cannot be evil because knives are simply tools which do not have free will and have many beneficial uses. Is it the blood flowing out from the wound made by the stabbing? Blood flowing is not evil. This is part of the natural laws of the physical world. What is evil is the action that we call murder; the process by which a murderer takes a knife and inserts it into an innocent victim's chest. However, this is not something that God made. God did not create the human being to be a murderer; rather, this is something the human being chose to do.

Another example is of a child who dies of cancer. We consider the death caused by cancer to be an evil. Did God cause this death by cancer? To answer this, let's analyze cancer. Cancer occurs when the cells in the body mutate and start to divide themselves in an unexpected fashion, which sometimes leads to the death of a patient. What part is evil? The cell? The splitting of the cell? The death? None of them! What is evil is the ignorance of the human being who has not yet been able to determine the cause of cancer. Again, it goes back to the human being's ignorance. Human ignorance is not caused by God, but rather by the human being himself.

A third example is earthquakes. When an earthquake takes place, hundreds or thousands of innocent people may die, and many people ask why God permitted this disaster to happen. Geologists say there are fault lines which stretch over the entire planet. These fault lines are a result of the active tectonic plates that have shaped our continents. Without tectonic plates, there would be no mountains, the earth would cool, and life would not be as diverse as it is. Land areas which are located near the fault lines are always at risk for earthquakes and have the potential to be destroyed. Some human beings choose to live near these fault lines with vulnerable homes. Again, it goes back to the ignorance of human beings—either ignorance about the fault lines, or ignorance in not protecting themselves by building earthquake-proof homes.

In certain countries, such as Japan, they have learned from mother-nature. Knowing that their country falls on fault lines, they build their homes and buildings in such a way that they absorb the quakes' shocks and therefore suffer many fewer causalities. An earthquake that measures seven on the Richter scale in Japan will result in much less damage than one of equal magnitude that may take place in Iran, Bangladesh, or Pakistan. Thus, the moving earth is not evil; and the earth's movement does not cause the people to die.

The second group of scholars, however, believes that God actually did create evil. They say is it not God who created the Devil and the evil-inclined soul that is constantly tempting us and enslaving us? God has created us in order to test us, and the presence of evil is an integral ingredient of this test.

Take a multiple-choice exam as an example. Each question has four or five answers to choose from, but there is only one right answer, and all of the other answers are incorrect. Who created and incorporated these wrong answers into the test? The professor or instructor. Why? In order to test the students.

An excellent way of testing them is to surround and envelop the right answer with wrong ones to determine who studied well and who did not. If all of the answers were correct, and no matter what the student chooses he or she would get it right, then it would not be a test!

Life is exactly the same. There is only one straight path to God (like the correct answer), and there is evil surrounding us in this life (like the wrong answers). The purpose of it all is to test us.

There are a number of Qur'anic verses which substantiate this view, such as chapter 76, verse 2.

12. Why do we need religion?

This is a question that is often asked. We have been created for a noble purpose. While some evolutionary scientists believe that humans are a mere accident or coincidence in the process of evolution, we believe that our life has a grand purpose. We are not simply the product of a natural, unintelligent process; rather, we have been designed by our Creator, God, and He has created us for an important cause. Religion drives our lives with a purpose. It is the tool which helps us achieve spirituality and completion; and which gives us direction and focus to achieve the purpose for which we were created. Since God is our Creator, He knows what is best for His creation, and thus, He gave us religion. A human being cannot truly fulfill the purpose of his creation without seeking guidance from his Creator.

Religion plays a major role in our lives. It is rooted in human history and psyche, and it is as old as human life. Scientists have demonstrated that religion is ingrained in our minds, and we have been essentially programmed to worship something Divine and Supernatural—and that is God. Religion helps us face and overcome our day to day challenges. It infuses our hearts with hope and protects us from falling into complete despair; and it confers upon us profound serenity and amazing tranquility. In our modern, hectic lives, as we are constantly battling anxiety and stress, especially in developed countries, religion remains a powerful source of comfort for all of us.

While academic institutions help us understand and grasp the natural world around us and enable us to achieve progress in various scientific fields, religion is primarily concerned with teaching us what is right and what is wrong. Simply put, it provides us with a beautiful moral standard. It helps us implement justice at the individual, family, social and global level. Religion serves to insulate us from committing crimes and spreading mischief. Furthermore, unlike any other institution, religion gives us a glimpse of what awaits us after we serve our life on earth, as it prepares us for the final judgment and eternal life. Finally, practicing religion is a way to thank God for the countless blessings which He has bestowed upon us.

A common misconception is that religion has historically been an impediment to scientific progress, and many wars were waged in the name of religion. While all religions throughout history have been misused by dictators, corrupt figures and evil groups to serve their own personal agendas, this does not mean that religion is bad. Humans have a tendency to misuse and exploit everything to serve their own interests. Money and power have always been misused, but that does not mean that they are bad. They are necessary for humanity's growth and progress, but they are misused because they have a reality behind them and carry a powerful driving force, and it is this reality and driving force that is exploited by many. The divine religion of God, similarly, is a reality and driving force in our lives, and therefore many have attempted to exploit it for their own evil interests. Science has also been exploited throughout history by various groups who pursue it for their own interests. More than ever, technology is being used to produce weapons of mass destruction. The weapons we have today have the potential to reduce the entire globe to absolute rubble in minutes.

The exploitation of religion does not diminish its value; rather, it makes us realize how significant it is in our lives and how we must strive to purify it from evil hands. It makes us aware that the battle to achieve justice is ongoing.

13. Do people have free will?

Free will is a very complex subject that has been debated for centuries amongst philosophers and Muslim scholars. The initial discussion over free will and predestination emerged about a century after the inception of Islam. Two Muslim groups, the *Mu'tazilites* and the *Asharites*, engaged in intense debates over free will and predestination.

The *Mu'tazilites* subscribed to the idea of absolute free will, as they believed that humans have full control over their fate and destiny without any intervention from God.

The exact opposite of the *Mu'tazilites* was a group known as the *Jabriyya*, or "hard determinists." They contended that humans are completely predestined and that they have no control over their fate and destiny. Therefore, they believed, the deviants have been predestined to their deviation, while the righteous have been predestined to their righteousness. If someone goes to the mosque to pray, he has been predestined and has no choice but to go to the mosque and pray; similarly, if a person goes to the bar and dances and drinks, then he too has no choice but to do so.

Although the *Asharites* seem to reject hard determinism, their conception of free will is not too different from the *Jabriyya*. Indeed some aspects of their views reveal that they are determinists. For example, they believe that God is the creator of human actions; and that every action we commit is directly created by God. Hence, while human beings make the intention to do good or bad, God is the one who creates their actions. To support this view, the *Asharites* cite some verses of the Qur'an, such as:

> *Surely you cannot guide whom you love, but God guides whom He pleases, and He knows best the followers of the right way.*[12]

---

[12] *Noble Qur'an*, Suratul Qasas (28), verse 56

Ultimately, they seem to subscribe to a form of determinism or predestination.

Most Muslim schools of thought today, such as the *Maliki*, *Hanbali*, *Shafi'i*, and *Hanafi*, subscribe to the *Asharite* view or at least adopt many aspects of it. The *Mu'tazilites*, on the other hand, no longer exist today.

The Shia school of thought stands in the middle of these two view-points. Imam Jafar al-Sadiq (a), the sixth Imam of the *Ahlul Bayt*, says, "It is neither coercion, nor abandonment; but it is a matter between the two." In other words, we are not completely predestined, nor do we have absolute free will. There are some aspects of our life over which we have no control, and there are other aspects which we do have control over.

A narration by Imam al-Sadiq (a) further explains:

> *Whatever you can blame the human being for - it is his action, and whatever you cannot blame him for - it is the act of God. God blames the human for committing sins, for wrongdoing, for drinking alcohol, committing adultery, etc. Thus, these are the acts of the person. However, God does not blame a person why he fell sick, why he was mentally ill, or why his skin color is black or white. Thus, these are the acts of God.* [13]

There are more subtle ways in which God has influence on our actions. For instance, if you are the type of person who generally has a good heart, wants the best for everyone, and strives to make the right intentions, then God will help you achieve good actions by removing any impediments that might get in your way. If you

---

[13] *Bihar al-Anwar*, vol. 5, p. 59, hadith 109

happen to make a decision to commit a sin or to wrong someone, then God might set an obstacle in your way that impedes you from committing that sin. On the contrary, if someone is evil-inclined and selfish, then God might "allow" him to commit a sin by not removing the obstacles that would prevent him from committing a sin. In both instances, we have free will and are in full control of our actions, but God has not abandoned us - rather, He supervises us, and wishes for us to make the right decisions.

Another narration sheds more light on the topic of free will:

People with regards to 'destiny' are of three categories: The first is a person who assumes that Allah has given full authority to him. This (person) has weakened God in His kingdom, thus, he is perished [the Mu'tazilites fall into this category]. The second is the one who assumes that God has forced people to sin and He has held them responsible for things over which they have no power. This (person) is unfair to God in His judgment, thus he is perished [the Jabriyya and a segment of the beliefs of the Asharites fall into this category]. The third is the one who assumes God has held people responsible for what they do and does not hold them responsible for what they have no power over. Therefore, when he does something good, he praises God and when he does something evil, he seeks God's forgiveness. This (person) is a mature Muslim. [14]

Given the complexity of free will and predestination, let us present an example to better understand these concepts.

Imagine you are driving a car and decide to crash into someone. We can analyze this incident in three ways:

---

[14] *Bihar al-Anwar*, vol. 5, p. 9, hadith 14

- The *Mu'tazilites*, who embrace complete free will, will tell you that God gave you the car, thus you are responsible for the accident, and God had no control over it. The accident is completely the result of your own free will.
- The *Asharites*, who embrace predestination, will tell you that God remotely controlled the car, and you really did not have much control over the accident. The accident is the direct result of God's will, as He created it.
- The Shia, however, believe that God gave you the car, and you are the one who decided to run into that person, but God still had control over the accident. If God wanted to save you from hitting that person, then He could have stopped you either by changing your mind or by placing an obstacle in your way that would have prevented you from killing the pedestrian. So we do have free will, but God can also intervene if He wants to.

From the Shia sources, we have some narrations which mention that we are predestined, but we must be clear on what is meant by these narrations.

Predestination from the Shia point of view does not mean that a person is coerced to a certain path; rather, it means that a person will be who he wants to be. For example, a medical student plans to be a doctor if he finishes his four years of study. If things go fine, then his college will grant him a degree in medicine four years after matriculation. But if he drops out, then he will not get that degree. This student is predestined to be a doctor *if* he follows through, meaning that he studies, does his homework, attends classes, and does what his instructors ask him to do. Then he will become a doctor.

When we speak about predestination from a philosophical point of view, the Shia Muslims believe that God predestined us to our own intentions and deeds. If someone strives to be a good person, then the outcome will depend on two factors:

- He must willingly strive to be a good person.
- God's blessings on him must create the conditions in which he can be a good person.

Therefore, the Shia do not consider predestination to be synonymous with coercion. Just because God knows our choices, it does not make it any less our choice.

Some might ask that from a religious perspective and the history of events in Islam, did God know that the murderer of Imam al-Husayn would commit such a crime, and if so, then why did He permit it to happen?

God definitely had full knowledge of the tragedy of Karbala before it occurred and that Imam al-Husayn and his family and friends would all be slaughtered. God also knew that the murderer would do so by his own free will. There are a number of reasons why God "allowed" for such a tragic event to take place.

First off, God wanted to elevate the status of Imam al-Husayn, and God will compensate him for every bit of suffering that he endured. The Prophet of Islam had foretold Imam al-Husayn that there was a special status in heaven that was reserved for him which could not be achieved except through his martyrdom.

Secondly, God wanted to punish people like Yazid who murdered Imam al-Husayn (a). Yazid was such an evil man who had a dark history of heinous crimes and wrongdoings, and by not stopping him from killing Imam al-Husayn (a), God ultimately allowed Yazid to deserve eternal damnation.

Finally, the tragedy of Karbala served as a powerful awakening to the Muslim nation in history and still serves as a catalyst up until now to awaken people to stand up against oppression and tyranny. Had God intervened in his tragic historical event, the Muslim world would have lost out on gleaming role-models and life-lessons on how and when to stand up to tyranny and injustice.

14. How can I develop a love for God?

If we remember the infinite number of favors that God has bestowed upon us, how much mercy He showers us with, and how tolerant and patient He is with us even though we disobey Him and sin so many times every day, then it will be very easy to find love for Him in our hearts.

In Du'a al-Iftitah, a very beautiful supplication (*du'a*) that is most commonly recited during the blessed Month of Ramadhan (9th month of the Muslim lunar calendar), there is a passage which explains how loving and caring God is to us:

> O Lord, You give me an invitation but I turn it down. You become familiar with me but I do not care for You. You love me but I do not correspond to You, as if You are overreaching me. Yet You do not abstain from bestowing favors and blessings on me from Your mercy and generosity; so have mercy on Your ignorant servant, Verily You are generous and kind.

An excellent way to learn how to love God is to remember that everything in this world is temporary and will eventually vanish.

All of the wealth that we possess, those whom we love, everything that we are attached to will one day perish. The only Being that will always remain, who is infinite and permanent, is God. Therefore, it makes sense to love that which has always been there and will never perish.

We can begin to show our love for God by waking up in the middle of the night, when everyone else is asleep, and initiate a humble and private conversation with God. We can reflect upon the bounties that He has showered us with, the mercy that He has encompassed us with, and how loving He is to us. In this way, we will begin our journey of closeness to Him and establish a true love for Him.

15. What is the gravest sin that a person can commit? Will God still forgive a person who commits that sin?

Muslims scholars divide sins into two categories: large-scale or major sins (*kabeera*) and small-scale or minor sins (*sagheera*).

In the first category, they list murder, adultery, drinking liquor, being disrespectful to parents, lying, theft, back-biting and gambling, among others. Some have added severing of relations with kinship, running away from the enemy while on the battlefield, and fleeing from legitimate sacred struggle (*jihad*) - one that is ordered by the Prophet Muhammad (ṣ) or one of the infallible 12 Imams. Scholars believe that these are among the gravest sins that a person can commit.

According to the Qur'an, the greatest sin is ascribing a partner to God:

> *Surely God does not forgive that anything should be associated with Him, and He forgives what is besides this to whom He pleases; and whoever associates anything with God, he indeed strays off into a remote error.*[15]

This is a sin that God, according to the Qur'an, does not forgive unless the person repents by fully believing in God.

There are scholars who believe that there is no such thing as big or small sins: all sins are big (because they are acts of disobedience to God), but some sins are relatively bigger than others.

Imam Ali (a) offers an interesting definition: "The gravest sin in the eyes of God is the one that a person takes lightly or disregards." A person seeking piety should refrain from committing any sin.

There are certain narrations that indicate that an individual should avoid all kinds of sins, for God has put His anger in some of these sins. Therefore, we should not risk committing any sin that may trigger God's anger since we do not know which sins they are.

Islamically, we believe that there is no sin that God will not forgive if one truly asks for forgiveness and repents.

Imam Zain al-Abideen (a), the fourth successor of Prophet Muhammad (ṣ) and a member of the Ahlul Bayt, saw a man clinging to the covering over the Ka'aba and asking the Lord to forgive him, but also saying that he knew the Lord would not forgive him. The Imam looked at him sternly and said: "Woe to

---

[15] *Noble Qur'an* Suratul Nisa (4), verse 116

you. I fear for your sense of hopelessness more than I fear the sin that you have committed."

To be hopeless of God's mercy or to believe that He will not forgive us is a major sin in Islam, because it amounts to rejecting God's mercy and power, as forgiveness shows God's mercy and compassion.

God, in numerous verses in the Qur'an, gives good news to the repentant and tells them that He is willing to embrace them and forgive them no matter what sins they have committed:

Say: O my servants who have acted extravagantly against their own souls, do not despair of the mercy of God; surely God forgives the faults altogether; surely He is the Forgiving, the Merciful.[16]

However, there are certain actions that will bring about worldly repercussions even if God forgives that person. Take as an example a thief who stole people's property - even if God forgives him, he must return the property that he stole. As for someone who killed an innocent person and repented to God, God may eventually forgive him; however, this person has to stand a worldly trial in which he may face capital punishment. God's forgiveness is for His judgment in the hereafter, but justice must be fulfilled in this world as well, even if it means capital punishment.

---

[16] *Noble Qur'an*, Suratul Zumar (39), verse 53

16. What are the conditions and requirements for a good friend?

Imam Ali (a) answered this question in his maxim to his son Imam Hasan (a). Imam Ali (a) instructed his son to choose a friend using the following criteria:

1. Do not befriend a fool, for he may want to benefit you, but he may end up hurting you instead.

2. Do not befriend the stingy or frugal person, for he will let you down when you are at your most difficult time.

3. Do not befriend a corrupt (or sinful) person, for he will sell you for a cheap price.

4. Do not befriend a liar, for he will make what is far seem close, and what is close seem far (meaning he will confuse you and not show you the truth).

5. Do not befriend one who is not firm in his faith, for he will adorn to you his mischief and he will want you to be like him.

6. Do not befriend one who is not totally committed to the religion or faith. He has no loyalty in his faith, and so he will steal from your faith without you even noticing or realizing it.[17]

In another narration, Imam Ali (a) encourages us to choose friends with the following quality: "Your true friend is the one who is honest with you, not someone who condones all of your actions." Friends who truly care about you are honest with you. If they realize that you are doing something wrong, then they will be kind

---

[17] *Nahj al-Balagha*, short sayings, maxim no. 38

enough to point that out to you. They will say what you need to hear, not necessarily what you would like to hear. Superficial friends, on the other hand, are not honest with you - when they realize that you are doing something wrong, they will make no effort to let you know. They will pamper and flatter you, and say only that what you like to hear.

Friends have so much influence on us that in one verse of the Qur'an, God indicates that part of the reason that the evil doers will be doomed to hell is because they chose bad or evil friends. God states:

> And the day when the unjust one will bite his hands saying: O I wish I had taken a way with the Messenger! O woe to me! I wish I had not taken such a one for a friend! Certainly he led me astray from the reminder after it had come to me; and Satan (the devil) fails to aid man.[18]

These verses reveal how significant it is for us to be selective of the friends that we have chosen, for they have an unparalleled influence upon us. A good friend may lead his friend in the right direction, while an unrighteous friend may not only lead his friend in the wrong direction, but maybe towards even a catastrophic end as well. We personally know good individuals who associated with irresponsible friends, and through their mischief, negligence, and heedlessness, caused an otherwise good person's tragic demise.

---

[18] *Noble Qur'an*, Suratul Furqan (25), verses 27–29

The Qur'an

17. How can one prove that the Qur'an is the Word of God?

Each prophet who claimed prophethood and received revelation from God was required to offer a miracle that proved the authenticity of his claim. Prophet Muhammad's (ṣ) miracles were numerous, but the greatest was the one that transcended time and geography: that being the Qur'an. In it, God even issued a challenge to all of humankind to bring forth a book that can compare to the Qur'an:

> *Say: If people and jinn should combine together to bring the like of this Qur'an, they cannot bring the like of it, though some of them were aiders of others.*[19]

God later challenged the world to create even a single chapter equal to the Qur'an:

> *And if you are in doubt as to that which We have revealed to Our servant, then produce a chapter like it and call on your witnesses besides God if you are truthful. But if you do (it) not and never shall you do (it), then be on your guard against the fire of which people and stones are the fuel; it is prepared for the unbelievers.*[20]

---

[19] *Noble Qur'an*, Suratul Isra (17), verse 88

[20] *Noble Qur'an*, Suratul Baqarah (2), verses 23–24

It has been fourteen centuries since God challenged humanity to match even a single chapter of the Qur'an and no one on earth has been able to meet this challenge.

The Qur'an is a miracle by all standards, but we prove it by the following three points:

1. The Qur'an contains the highest level of Arabic eloquence, a level that no Arab poet, regardless of his or her talent, has ever been able to come close to.

The miracle of Prophet Moses (a) was consistent with the prevalent customs of his time: magic and 'sleight of hand.' What he provided by way of his miracle, however, was far beyond what society was able to produce. No magician could reproduce his miracle of transforming his stick into a colossal snake and his miracle of splitting the sea.

Prophet Jesus (a) produced his miracles, such as curing the sick, healing the ill, and bringing the dead back to life, at a time when medicine was most valuable.

In Prophet Muhammad's (ṣ) lifetime, the most popular phenomena were poetry and eloquence, and therefore, his miracle was in line with the requirements of his era and surpassed everything else in existence, and will continue to do so until the end of time.

2. The Qur'an is a miracle in its prophecies. In many instances, the Qur'an made prophecies that were soon fulfilled. One conspicuous example is where it is foretold:

The Romans are vanquished, In a near land, and they, after being vanquished, shall overcome, Within a few years. God's is the command before and after; and on that day the believers shall rejoice.[21]

The verses were in reference to a battle that took place between the Persian Empire and the Roman Empire in 614–615 for the land of Jerusalem. Within a few years, as the Qur'an stated, the Romans, under the leadership of Heraclius, defeated the Persian Empire in 622 at a battle called Issus.

Another prophecy the Qur'an made was Prophet Muhammad's (ṣ) victory over the pagans of Mecca. When the pagans of Mecca waged a war against the Muslims and banned them from visiting the Grand Mosque in Mecca, defeating the pagans seemed to be only a dream for many of Medina's Muslims. The Qur'an however, instilled hope into their hearts by promising them that they would triumphantly enter the Grand Mosque and perform the *Hajj*, or the holy pilgrimage.[22] Very soon after, this prophecy materialized.

3. Scientific facts proven since the Prophet's time demonstrate the Qur'an's superiority in scientific fields.

But nay! I swear by the Lord of the Easts and the Wests that We are certainly able.[23]

This verse was revealed at a time when Meccans believed the earth was flat. Therefore, there would have been only one east and one west. Only if the earth was round would it have been comprehensible to think of "easts" and "wests." As the sun rises at one point for those observing it from the west, it is also setting at

---

[21] *Noble Qur'an*, Suratul Room (30), verses 2–4

[22] *Noble Qur'an*, Suratul Fath (48), verse 27

[23] *Noble Qur'an*, Suratul Ma'arij (70), verse 40

the same time for those living further east. Then it can rise later on in a different area, making a different east. This fact was not empirically proven until 1522, when some in Ferdinand Magellan's crew first circumnavigated the earth. This verse is vivid proof on the roundness of the earth at a time when many still believed that it was flat.

Another common theory at the time of the Qur'an's revelation was that the earth is stationary and that the sun revolves around the earth. In the Qur'an, God defeats this theory through the following verse:

Have We not made the earth an even expanse (mehaad)?[24]

In addition to "expanse," many scholars interpret the Arabic word *mehaad* as a rocking surface in which a child is often put in where he comfortably enjoys his sleep.

The resemblance of the earth to a child's cradle is a reference to the rocking or movement of the earth that has been proven scientifically with a calculated speed of about 1,037 miles/hour at the equator (the closer you get to the poles the slower the speed becomes). Just like a child enjoys sleep and does not feel the rocking, humans enjoy their livelihood on earth without feeling the movement of the earth.

Another example of the Qur'an's scientific understanding is the following:

Do not those who disbelieve see that the heavens and the earth were closed up, but We have opened them; and We have made of water every living thing, will they not then believe?[25]

---

[24] *Noble Qur'an*, Suratul Naba (78), verse 6

This verse meets the most updated scientific finding about the creation of the universe, something known as the Big Bang Theory. The Big Bang Theory asserts that the universe expanded into its current state from a primordial mass of enormous density and temperature. From this explosion, all of the galaxies and solar systems, including the earth and other planets in our solar system, were created. The Qur'an clearly indicates in this verse that the earth was part of the sun (closed up) before God separated them. Then the earth became an independent planet.

One final example of the scientific truths in the Qur'an is the below:

And the sun runs on to a term appointed for it; that is the ordinance of the Mighty, the Knowing.[26] Neither is it allowable to the sun that it should overtake the moon, nor can the night outstrip the day; and all float on in a sphere.[27]

These verses speak about the sun having two different and distinct motions; spinning about on its axis and moving about in the galaxy. In the first verse, God speaks about the sun spinning about its axis. In the second verse, God speaks about the sun moving around in the galaxy. These are scientific facts not commonly known until more recent times, facts that the Qur'an mentioned 1,400 years ago, proving the timelessness and authenticity of its revelation.

---

[25] *Noble Qur'an*, Suratul Anbiya (21), verse 30
[26] *Noble Qur'an*, Suratul Yaseen (36), verse 38
[27] *Noble Qur'an*, Suratul Yaseen (36), verse 40

There are many other scientific breakthroughs in the Qur'an which attest to its authenticity, such as the stages of fetal development,[28] the fact that water is the source of all life,[29] and other realities about our universe.

From all of these evidences, we can conclude that the Qur'an has been revealed by God and God alone, and the further we go from the time of revelation, the more we find science supporting the Qur'an. This is why Imam al-Sadiq (a) said: "The Qur'ans astonishment will never vanish, and its wonders will never end."[30]

It is important to note, however, that while the Qur'an contains a plethora of scientific facts, it is not a book of science. It is, most importantly, a book of guidance for all of humankind.

18. When was the Qur'an put into the book form as we know it today?

According to narrations from the Ahlul Bayt, the Qur'an was compiled in its current form and sequence during the life of Prophet Muhammad (ṣ). The Prophet assigned Imam Ali (a) to compile it.

Many Muslim scholars believe that the Qur'an was revealed to the Prophet with seven systems of pronunciation, meaning that some words were revealed with multiple pronunciations depending on the vowel markings. These pronunciations are all

---

[28] *Noble Qur'an*, Suratul Mo'minoon (23), verses 12–14, and Suratul Zumar (39) verse 6

[29] *Noble Qur'an*, Suratul Anbiya (21), verse 30

[30] *Al-Amali* of Shaykh al-Sadouq, p. 366

legitimate, as certain Arabic words can have more than one pronunciation and still carry an acceptable meaning.

During the reign of the third Caliph, Uthman, there appeared more than one copy with slight differences in pronunciation. Uthman decided to eliminate all of the copies except one of them, and the one he chose was according to the way that Hafs ibn Asim recited or pronounced it. Unfortunately, he burned all of the other copies and only allowed the Muslims to read the copy he had chosen. Uthman believed that this would unify the Muslim community (*ummah*). However, many others argued that it was not up to Uthman to eliminate the legitimate readings or pronunciations of the Qur'an under any circumstances. The current Qur'an that Muslims read is basically the one that Uthman had chosen, which is why you can find in many of the present day copies of the Qur'an the words *"Mushaf Uthman."*

19. What is the rationale behind the Qur'an's structure, since some parts of a verse (*ayat*) were not revealed at the same time as the rest of the same verse?

According to Muslim scholars, the order in which the Qur'an appears today is the same order which Prophet Muhammad (ṣ) himself ordered his companions to compile it in.

We know some of the reasons for the compilation in this present format, and some we do not. Perhaps the flow, the relevance of a subject, and the magnificence of the Qur'an could not have been achieved without the order which the Prophet himself designed - by God's decree.

With respect to its current sequence and structure, the Qur'an has two objectives: the first was to guide those early Muslims who witnessed significant and perilous events, and the second was to guide the later generations that would come. Hence, revealing individual verses or sets of verses relevant to those events benefited the first group, while designing the Qur'an in the current book form which we have benefits the second group.

We must remember that Muslims faced extremely difficult challenges during Islam's early stages and up until Prophet Muhammad's (ṣ) death. Countless battles were waged against them, numerous groups and tribes conspired against them, and they could have been eradicated in a blink of an eye.

In the Battle of Badr, for instance, Muslims numbered only 313 and only had seventy camels and two horses. The Meccan pagans, on the other hand, mobilized 950 fighters with hundreds of camels and horses. Initially, the Muslims seemed no match for them. One of the ways that God strengthened the faith, resolve and determination of the Muslims was by revealing individual verses that directly addressed such important events. This allowed those early Muslims to interact with the Qur'an and engage with the verses much more effectively, and that was how they achieved victory. Had the Qur'an been revealed at once in the current sequence and form that we have, it would not have had this great effect.

However, as Islam gained victory and prevailed, God instructed the Prophet to compile the Qur'an into one book that would continue to inspire everyone, especially the later generations.

Thus, the form which we have in our hands and dates back to the era of the Prophet is truly an awe-inspiring format.

We can compare the Qur'an to a magnificent building in which all of the material required to construct the building are brought to the work site in what may seem to us to be a random order. However once the construction workers and engineers, using the plans and blue-prints, assembled the structure, it ends up resembling the breath-taking building which the architect had envisioned it to be.

The verse revealed at the beginning of Islam, chapter 96, verse 1, is found near the end of the Qur'an:

Read in the name of your Lord Who created.[31]

In the same way, verses that were revealed in the last days of Prophet Muhammad's (ṣ) life are in the beginning of the Qur'an.

Historians believe that the last verse revealed to the Prophet was chapter 5, verse 3, which reads:

This day have I perfected for you your religion and completed My favor on you and chosen for you Islam as a religion.[32]

20. Does it suffice to read the Qur'an in English?

In its original Arabic form, the Qur'an is the direct word of God. In translation, however, it is the work of humans and loses its unique style and power – in any language in which it is translated. Different translators, for example, may interpret some verses differently.

It is still beneficial to read the Qur'an in English in order to understand its general contents, but anyone who encounters what

---

[31] *Noble Qur'an*, Suratul Alaq (96), verse 1

[32] *Noble Qur'an*, Suratul Ma'idah (5), verse 3

seems to be a contradiction, an inconsistency, or an ambiguity should ask the experts who will be able to carefully refer to the original Arabic text to understand the true meanings.

It goes without saying that mastering Arabic is the best way to learn the traditions of Prophet Muhammad (ṣ) and his family and interpret the Qur'anic verses in the best possible way.

21. Is there a verse in the Qur'an that speaks about God appointing Imam Ali (a) as the caliph directly after Prophet Muhammad (s)?

The Qur'an has many verses indicating or hinting that God appointed Imam Ali (a) as Prophet Muhammad's (ṣ) rightful caliph immediately after his death. While the name of Imam Ali (a) is not explicitly mentioned in the Qur'an, many verses do refer to him being appointed the caliph. Two such verses are as follows:

> O Messenger! Deliver what has been revealed to you from your Lord; and if you do not do it, then you have not delivered His message, and God will protect you from the people; surely God will not guide the unbelieving people.[33]

In this verse, God commands the Prophet to deliver a very important message to the people. This verse was revealed shortly before the incident of Ghadir Khum, where the Prophet, in compliance to God's command, stopped all of his companions and followers in the middle of the desert and formally appointed Imam Ali (a) as his successor. At Ghadir Khumm, God ordered the

---

[33] *Noble Qur'an*, Suratul Ma'idah (5), verse 67

Prophet to tell the people that Imam Ali (a) will be his successor appointed by God.

Another verse in the Qur'an also confirms that Imam Ali (a) was the Prophet's successor and the authority after him:

*Only God is your Patron and His Messenger and those who believe, those who keep up prayers and pay the charity **while** they bow.*[34]

This verse states that the only rightful guardians of humankind are God, Prophet Muhammad (s), and the believers who pray and pay alms **while** they bow.

The word *patron* in this verse means *leader* or *ruler,* and all of the scholars have stated that the "believers who pray and pay alms while they bow" refers only to Imam Ali (a), as the verse is about a specific historical event that occurred when a poor man asked Imam Ali (a) for help while the Imam was praying. The Imam gave his ring to the poor man while he was bowing in the prayer. Since this verse states that Islam has only three leaders, it is proof that Imam Ali (a) is the rightful leader of the Muslims, appointed by God, and that Muslims must follow and obey him, as they obey God and the Prophet.

There are many other verses of the Qur'an and narrations that prove Imam Ali (a) was the rightful Caliph immediately after the death of the Prophet and appointed by God, but the two mentioned should suffice to identify Imam Ali (a) as the rightful Caliph.

---

[34] *Noble Qur'an,* Suratul Ma'idah (5), verse 55

22. Did Prophet Muhammad (s) appoint Imam Ali (a) to scribe the Qur'an?

There is a great number of traditions from both the Sunni and Shia sources stating that after the death of Prophet Muhammad (ṣ), Imam Ali (a) swore an oath that he would not don his outdoor clothes or leave his house until he gathered all of the revelations of the Qur'an into one book.

The Noble Qur'an was compiled during the Prophet's life, but since many of the chapters and verses were scribed on individual pieces of paper and thus somewhat scattered, Imam Ali (a) gathered all of those verses and compiled them into a complete book. This is something which Imam Ali (a) was directly instructed do to by the Prophet, and he carried it out immediately after Prophet Muhammad (ṣ) passed away.

Some Sunni references which highlight this fact include:

1. *Fath al-Bari fi Sharh Sahih al-Bukhari* by Ibn Hajar al-Asqalani, volume 10, page 386

2. *Al-Itqan* by al-Suyuti, volume 1, page 165

3. *Al-Masahif* by Ibn Abi Dawud, page 10

4. *Al-Sawa'iq al-Muhriqah* by Ibn Hajar al-Haythami, chapter 9, section 4, page 197

5. *Ma'rifat al-Qurra' al-Kibar* by al-Dhahabi, volume 1, page 31

23. Why do none of the holy books speak about dinosaurs?

The Qur'an does not speak about dinosaurs, just like it does not speak about the native Indians. God also does not speak about the pyramids in Egypt, the Yamo Yamo civilization in ancient Latin

America, the Great Wall of China, or about Japan's Mount Fuji. God avoided mentioning things that might make the Qur'an seem like a geography, biography, or history book.

Even though the Qur'an does contain stories and parables of ancient nations, it generally stayed away from certain specifics such as the names and locations of individuals. Simply stated, the Qur'an is a book of guidance, and since speaking about dinosaurs is not so relevant to guiding humanity, there was no need to mention them. The Qur'an invites us to contemplate the creation of God, be amazed at the wonders of His creation, and consequently better grasp God's greatness so we draw ourselves closer to Him. When studying dinosaurs, we must remind ourselves of God's greatness.

Islamic History

24. Did Prophet Adam (a) sin by eating the "forbidden fruit"?

The story of Prophet Adam (a) and the forbidden tree is one that has been greatly debated amongst the three monotheistic religions. Christianity considers the story to be the basis of the original sin which humanity inherited from Adam (a), and it places the blame on Eve (a).[35] Christianity is based on the original sin, and Prophet Jesus (a) was sent to save humanity from this sin.[36]

Islam however, views this story differently.

First off, the Qur'an holds Adam (a) and Eve (a) both responsible for eating from the forbidden tree.[37]

Secondly, Islam does not accept the idea of the original sin. Even if we assume that Prophet Adam (a) sinned, it is unjust for God to hold humanity accountable for a sin they did not commit; and it would also be unjust for God to have Prophet Jesus (a) expiate a sin which he never committed in the first place. The religion of Islam states that God holds us all accountable only for the sins that we commit ourselves and not for the sins of others.

Third, and most importantly, it is pertinent to note that the prophets chosen by God to lead humanity do not commit any sins at all. If they did commit a sin, then this would imply that God

---

[35] *Bible,* 1 Timothy 2:14

[36] *Bible,* 1 John 4:10

[37] *Noble Qur'an,* Suratul A'raf (7), verses 20-22

condones sinning because He ordered us to follow these individuals. Therefore, Muslim scholars throughout history have agreed that no prophet has ever committed a sin. What appears to be a "sin" is rather a less favored choice of God. Hence, the concept of "sinning" is relative. What is merely inadvisable for us to do may be considered a sin if a prophet does it, and according to Qur'anic literature, a "less favored choice of God" can be referred to as an act of disobedience, but technically, it is not a sin.

If we analyze the story of Prophet Adam (a), we come to realize that he did not commit a sin. The Qur'an asserts that when God informed the angels about His intent to create Adam (a), He said: "I will create a deputy on earth." [38] But then God created Adam (a) in heaven, not on earth, which reveals that Adam (a) did not sin and was not expelled from heaven because he "sinned." God's intent to create him on earth illustrates that from the onset, God's objective was to place Adam (a) and his offspring on earth, and sending him to earth was not a punishment. Being placed on the Earth was simply a matter of time, and God had left it up to Adam (a) to decide when his earthly trials would begin. God had advised him, however, that if he ate from the forbidden tree, there would be hard consequences. Adam (a) could have remained in heaven longer – a place in which he experienced no pain or difficulty – if he would not have eaten from the tree; but doing so expedited the start of his test.

Furthermore, when Adam (a) descended to earth, he constantly wept and invoked God's forgiveness. God forgave him, but He did not send him back to paradise. Had Adam (a) committed a sin and

---

[38] *Noble Qur'an*, Suratul Baqarah (2), verse 30

consequently been expelled from paradise, God should have sent him back to paradise after forgiving him. Keeping him on the earth, however, is proof that Adam's (a) action did not constitute a sin.

One may then wonder that if it was not a sin, then what was it? Prophet Adam (a) did not deliberately and defiantly eat from the tree; rather, Satan lured and tricked him. At that moment, Adam (a) forgot that the devil was his enemy and thought that he was offering him good advice. Satan took an oath in God that he was giving Adam (a) good advice. It had never been precedented for Adam (a) that anyone would take a false oath in God. It never crossed his mind that Satan would take a false oath in God. From the Qur'an we read:

And certainly We gave a commandment to Adam before, but he forgot; and We did not find in him determination.[39]

God had advised him that if he desired to stay in heaven, then he should abstain from approaching the forbidden tree. But if he wanted to descend to earth where he would face many difficulties, then he could eat from the tree. Adam (a) simply did not take God's advice, and that is what the Qur'an meant by saying that Adam (a) disobeyed God and lacked determination. Had he been fully determined to stay in heaven, then he would have avoided the tree.

God tells us about the story of the forbidden tree to remind us that Satan, the devil, is our avowed enemy. His entire goal in his existence is to lure us and set up traps for us; and therefore we

---

[39] *Noble Qur'an*, Suratul Taha (20), verse 115

must take him as an enemy and resist the temptations he creates for us. Just as Satan tried to trick the first parents of humanity, Adam (a) and Eve (a), he will also try to misguide all of humanity. We must always be on guard to ensure that we remain away from him and obedient to God.

25. How can Prophet Muhammad (s) and his family (*the Ahlul Bayt*) have been created before all of humankind?

The first narration in the book of *al-Kafi*, by al-Kulayni, sheds some light on this question. It states that the most beloved creation of God is the intellect; and this intellect is the vehicle through which God is worshipped and through which His greatness is appreciated. Other narrations point out that the intellect was God's first creation.

The full and complete intellect is embodied and personified by Prophet Muhammad (ṣ) and the Imams of the Ahlul Bayt. This is one way of understanding how Prophet Muhammad (ṣ) and the Imams were God's first creation.

In *Ziyarat al-Jame'a*, which is a visitation addressing the noble Imams of Ahlul Bayt narrated from Imam al-Hadi (a), the tenth Imam of Ahlul Bayt, there is a passage that says:

And (God) created you [in the beginning] lights that surrounded His throne.

Prophet Muhammad (ṣ) has also said in a narration: "The first thing God created was my light."[40] The essence and exact nature of this light is not known to us, and some scholars believe that this

---

[40] *Bihar al-Anwar*, vol. 1, p. 97, hadith 7

light symbolizes the complete intellect. Another narration from the Prophet substantiates the fact that the Ahlul Bayt were the first of God's creation. It states:

> The first thing that God, the Almighty and Glorified, created was our souls. Then God caused us to declare His oneness and glorify Him. Then He created the angels after us.[41]

One may assume that there is an apparent contradiction among these narrations, as some state that God first created their light, while others state that He first created their souls, and yet other narrations tell us that God first created the intellect. However, in reality, there is no discrepancy here. In essence, all of these narrations refer to a single reality, and this reality is manifested in the noble Prophet and his Ahlul Bayt. The light, the soul and the intellect are all simply different dimensions of a single reality.

26. Why did Prophet Muhammad (s) marry multiple women?

Prophet Muhammad (ṣ) was not just a prophet - he was a statesman, a community father figure, and the guardian of society, as well as a great teacher. None of his marriages were aimed at fulfilling lusts or physical desires, for the Prophet stood above allowing physical desires and urges rule his life.

In his first marriage to Lady Khadija (a), the Prophet aimed to form a family and have a normal marital life. In this period of his life, he was married only to one woman. After her death, his other

---

[41] *Uyoon Akhbar al-Redha*, vol. 1, p. 262, hadith 22

marriages served noble intentions, which varied from political to social reasons.

The Arabian Peninsula was rampant with raiding and pillaging at the time. One great mechanism that the Prophet used to bring peace and tranquility to the society was allying with tribes that were relentlessly fighting each other and resisting the new civil order which he had established. One way to achieve that was to marry a woman from certain tribes and thus dissuade them from fighting. This was the case for him marrying Juwayreya bint al-Harith who came from a prominent tribe. Through his marriage to her, the Prophet ultimately persuaded her tribe not to fight any further.

Another reason the Prophet married some of the women was to break down divisions between the various monotheistic religions, and so he formed a bond between Islam and Christianity and between Islam and Judaism.

Unfortunately, some Christians and Jews during his time were involved in plots against the Prophet, which in turn resulted in hard feelings for some Muslims toward the Jews and Christians. The Prophet attempted to dispel any potential hatred in the hearts of Muslims and reached out to the Jews and Christians.

One way of achieving this was by marrying Marya (Mary) the Coptic. She was, interestingly, the only wife other than Khadija (a) to have children with the Prophet. She was the mother of Abraham (a), their child, who died at a very young age in his infancy. Even though Marya the Coptic converted to Islam, her parents remained Christians. The Prophet's marriage to this lady helped Muslims and Christians resolve their differences.

The same motivation applied to Safia bint Hoyay bin Akhtab, a Jew who traced her ancestry to Prophet Aaron (a), the brother of Prophet Moses (a). Some Jews in Medina had been involved in a conspiracy against the Prophet. He asked them to leave Medina, and they settled in the northern part of the Arabian Peninsula, but they continued in their plans to overthrow the government of Medina. In response, the Prophet conquered their fortress, Khaybar. However, careful not to inflame Muslim-Jewish relations, the Prophet married the Jewish Safia, who converted to Islam, to tamp down any resentment among the Muslims.

Certain narrations mention that Ayesha, another wife of the Prophet, would often tease Safia by calling her names and making light of her Jewishness. Safia consulted the Prophet for advice, and he reminded her that she was the wife of a prophet and the descendant of a prophet. Her grandfather, Aaron (a) was a prophet, and her great-uncle Moses (a), was also a prophet. Safia would then tell Ayesha this, and thus, Ayesha kept quiet.

The Prophet married Ayesha, the daughter of Abu Bakr, who later assumed power as the first Caliph after the Prophet's death, to help neutralize his opponents within the Quraysh - the powerful tribe in Mecca that originally opposed him. Abu Bakr came from a prominent sub-tribe of the Quraysh called Taim.

The Prophet married some other women simply because these women had no one else to take care of them. This was the case with Umm Habeeba, the daughter of Abu Sufiyan, the leader of the pagans in Mecca. She and her husband, Abdullah bin Jahsh, were among the early Muslims who migrated to Ethiopia to escape persecution from the Meccans. In Ethiopia, her husband defected and converted to Christianity; and thus, she was left alone to face an ambiguous future without the support of anyone as her father was a zealous pagan. The Prophet learned about her situation, and in the absence of an established welfare and social-security system, he found no other solution to protect this lady other than to marry her.

Widows often found it difficult to remarry, but these were many women who frequently became widowed because of the several battles and wars during that period of time. The Prophet was aware of the responsibility of the Muslims to protect them. He married Umm Salama after she lost her husband in the Battle of Uhud. She narrated that one day, long after the death of her husband, the Prophet came to see her. He asked for her hand in marriage knowing that she even had children whom she had to care for. She narrated that in the beginning, she hesitated because she did not want her children to disturb the Prophet. However, the Prophet replied that her children will be like his own, and he will take care of them. Umm Salama indicated to the Prophet that she was not a young woman whom he would enjoy and that she did not have much to offer him. The Prophet replied that he too was old, and that he was not marrying her for her youthfulness or her beauty, but rather because she was a widow struggling to raise children on her own. [42]

This shows that the Prophet was fulfilling the role of a father figure in the Muslim community. He was very conscious about protecting those who needed his protection.

---

[42] *Al-Isabah*, vol. 8, p. 406

He proved it again with Hafsa, the daughter of Omar bin al-Khattab, the man who would later become the second Caliph. After Hafsa's husband died while she was still young, her father approached numerous companions asking them to marry her; however none of them accepted. Omar came to the Prophet crying that nobody would accept his daughter in marriage. He particularly complained about the last man that he had approached, Othman bin Affan, later the third Caliph. The Prophet replied that Hafsa will marry a man better than Othman, and he then married Hafsa simply because she had nobody else to take care of her.

One of the Prophet's marriages helped to break a false, long-standing Arab tradition. At the Prophet's request, his cousin Zaynab bint Jahsh married his adopted son Zayd bin Haritha. Zayd was a young man who was brought as a slave to Mecca before Islam and was sold in the market. The Prophet had purchased him, freed him, and then adopted him. Unfortunately, Zaynab and Zayd could not get along and they got divorced. Later, God abolished adoptions in Islam by asking people not to claim their adopted children as their own children and attribute them to the adopting parents. Rather, Islam instructed that adopted children be attributed to their biological parents. To underscore this change, God ordered the Prophet to marry Zaynab, the divorcée of his adopted son.

Under the old tradition, this would not have been allowed, (and even now it is not permitted for a man to marry his daughter-in-law if she divorces his son) but this new marriage showed that Zayd was not actually the Prophet's son.

The Prophet lived in a monogamous relationship with Khadija for twenty-five years, but his later marriages all served one noble cause or another, whether it was humanitarian, educational, political, or social.

A strong indication which demonstrates that he did not marry to fulfill his personal desires is the offer that the pagans in Mecca had presented him with. They promised him that if he relinquishes preaching Islam, then they would declare him their king and would give him many of their most beautiful women. The Prophet utterly rejected this and said to them: "if [you] put the sun in my right hand and the moon in my left hand so that I abandon my mission, I will never do so until my mission prevails or I die conveying it."

If the Prophet wanted to fulfill his personal desires of marrying women, then he would have taken this golden opportunity. But his goal was to simply convey the message of God, and he never made a single effort in his life to fulfill his personal whims or desires. All of his marriages were for the sake of God and the betterment of Islam. Those who accuse him of having other motives are ignorant and narrow-minded.

27. Some accounts say that Prophet Muhammad (s) married Ayesha when she was nine years old – is this true?

Historical records only show that Prophet Muhammad (ṣ) married Ayesha. There are no authentic sources or documents that establish her definite age at the time. Accounts narrated by Ayesha herself claim that she was nine at the time of her marriage to the Prophet, but no other narrators from among the companions of the Prophet confirm these accounts. Thus, her accounts are questionable, if not dubious.

Furthermore, history reveals that Ayesha had a tendency to exaggerate her own qualities. She often implied that she was the most favored, beautiful, and desired wife of the Prophet, and many scholars suspect her claims of being married remarkably young as a means to confer special status to herself.

Muslim scholars who have reported that Ayesha was only nine at the time of her marriage relied solely on Ayesha's accounts.

Many of those scholars have accepted these historical narrations with good intentions; but without corroboration of her narrations, we cannot accept these ahadith as being true and authentic.

According to the research of some contemporary scholars, she was more likely somewhere between thirteen and seventeen years old at the time she got married.[43] These scholars have gathered some historical dates of the year of her birth and year of her death, and these records demonstrate that she could not have been nine years when the Prophet married her.

28. Why did Islam not abolish slavery in one instance?

In order to fully appreciate why Islam did not abolish slavery in one instance, one must understand life on the Arabian Peninsula at the time of Prophet Muhammad (ṣ). When he began to preach Islam in the year 610 AD, most of the world's economies, whether they were industrial or agricultural, relied heavily on slavery.

---

[43] Al-Sahih min al-Sirah, vol. 3, p. 285

Slaves made up the majority of the labor force in workshops and on farms, and many others were also warriors and soldiers.

The sources of enslavement were many. In some societies, unpaid debts entitled the lender to enslave the debtor. Under Jewish law, a thief could be enslaved by the victim of the theft. God tells us in the Qur'an (and it is also mentioned in the Book of Genesis of the Old Testament) that Prophet Joseph (a), who was Prophet Jacob's (a) son, planted the Egyptian king's cup in the bag of his younger brother Benjamin. Then Prophet Joseph (a) asked his brothers, who had not recognized him yet, what the penalty is for theft. They said that the thief would have to be enslaved. Someone then announced that the king's cup was missing, and they ultimately found it in Benjamin's bag. Consequently, Prophet Joseph (a) gained custody of Benjamin. From the Qur'an we read the following:

> So when he furnished them with their provisions, (someone) placed the drinking cup in his brother's bag. Then a crier cried out: O caravan! you are most surely thieves. They said while they were facing them: What is it that you miss? They said: We miss the king's drinking cup, and he who shall bring it will have a camel-load and I am responsible for it. They said: By God! you know for certain that we have not come to make mischief in the land, and we are not thieves. They said: But what shall be the requital of this, if you are liars? They said: The requital of this is that the person in whose bag it is found shall himself be (held for) the satisfaction thereof; thus do we punish the wrongdoers. So he began with their sacks before the sack of his brother, then he brought it out from his brother's sack. Thus did We plan for the sake of Joseph; it was not

(lawful) that he should take his brother under the king's law unless God pleased; We raise the degrees of whomsoever We please, and above every one possessed of knowledge is the All-Knowing One. They said: If he steals, a brother of his did indeed steal before; but Joseph kept it secret in his heart and did not disclose it to them. He said: You are in an evil condition and God knows best what you state.[44]

At the time of its introduction, Islam did not recognize any of the above-mentioned rationales for slavery, such as debt or theft, to be legitimate. But Islam had to be realistic about the third cause of slavery – which was wars. When Islam came into existence, there were no international treaties organizing the fate of prisoners of war. Capturing armies mostly enslaved them. Therefore, Islam had to face that reality; and thus Muslims would act accordingly and enslave their own prisoners of war.

This does not mean that Islam did not push to eliminate slavery – in fact it did. However, an abrupt abolishment of slavery would have meant paralyzing the economy and the lives of many slaves.

Thus, Islam gradually introduced ways to set slaves free. Prophet Muhammad (ṣ) set forth the following binding resolutions for freeing slaves.

1. If a female slave became pregnant by her master, then he was prohibited from selling her. He had to wait until she delivered their child. Once she delivered, if the child remained alive, then he still could not sell her, and upon the death of her master, she immediately became free.

---

[44] *Noble Qur'an*, Surat Yusuf (12), verses 70–77

2. A master who harshly mistreated his slave was required to free the slave immediately.

3. A slave could buy freedom by working for an amount of time and saving an amount of cash agreed upon with the master.

4. Islam discouraged the practice of *dhihar*, a notorious practice common among Arabs before Islam. If a man became extremely angry with his wife, then he would say to her, "You are to me like my mother," which meant that just as he would never marry or engage in a sexual relationship with his mother, he would also sever his relationship with his wife. This was considered a great insult to the wife. Upon saying this, his wife became forbidden to him, meaning that her husband could no longer sustain a marital relationship with her. Islam prohibited this tradition by mandating that a Muslim man who engaged in *dhihar* free a slave in order for his wife to become permissible for him again.

5. Breaking one's own fast intentionally in Islam required the person to fast for two months, feed sixty poor people, or set a slave free for each day the fast was broken. If this person broke a fast with something prohibited, like wine, then he had to fulfill all three penalties: fast for sixty days, feed sixty poor, and set a slave free. In addition, Islam constantly encouraged Muslims to set their own slaves free; and even indicated that those who set slaves free would be set free by God from hell on the Day of Judgment.

Imam Zain al-Abideen (a), the fourth Imam of Ahlul Bayt, reportedly bought slaves every year before the month of Ramadhan. He would educate and guide these slaves for one year; then during the following year, the Imam would give each one of these slaves remuneration to live on, and on the night of Eid al-Fitr (the end of the month of Ramadhan), he would set them all free. His treatment was reported to be so decent and gracious that some slaves insisted on remaining with him as slaves.

29. Did Prophet Muhammad (s) order the slaughtering of eight hundred Jews?

During the war of *Khandaq*, numerous parties and tribes joined forces against Prophet Muhammad (s) and the Muslim community. They had formed a formidable alliance to kill all Muslims.

Prior to the battle, the Jews of Banu Quraydha, a tribe living under Muslim protection within Medina, had concluded a treaty with Prophet Muhammad (s). According to its terms, they were supposed to remain neutral and not engage in any hostile acts against their hosts (meaning the Muslims). However, during that war, Banu Quraydha committed treason against Muslims by exposing their secrets, showing the enemies the weak spot of Medina and lending the enemies weapons, thereby enabling them to penetrate into Medina and kill many Muslims.

After the war, news of the treason was revealed, and the Prophet put the Jewish leaders of Banu Quraydha on trial. After they admitted their act of treason, the Prophet asked them whether they would prefer that he determine the sentence for them or another person pass the verdict. The Jews had a long-standing alliance and friendship with a prominent figure and companion of the Prophet, Saad bin Ma'adh, and so they chose him to be their arbitrator. The Prophet agreed and Saad then issued a death sentence for all of the adult Jews involved in the treason.

Most Muslim historians believe that the number did not exceed 350 men. The Prophet allowed the execution of these Jews not because they were Jewish or that he was driven by animosity toward the Jews, but because they engaged in treason.

Treason at that time was punishable by death, and in fact even today in many countries around the world this still holds true. The United States Code 18 U.S.C. § 2381 specifically stipulates death as a possible punishment for treason. In 1953, the U.S. executed the Rosenbergs for passing secrets to the Soviets.

30. Did Prophet Muhammad (s) order death for any Muslims that changed their religion?

The Qur'an is the best source for learning Islamic laws; and in it God states:

There is no compulsion in religion; truly the right way has become clearly distinct from error.[45]

We have no evidence that the Prophet ordered the death of any Muslim who changed his religion.

Historians do mention the story of Abdullah ibn Abi Sarh, who was a Muslim, a companion of the Prophet and a member of the Qur'an's writing committee. He defected from the religion, went to Mecca, and defamed the Prophet. The Prophet ordered his

---

[45] *Noble Qur'an*, Suratul Baqarah (2), verse 256

execution—not for changing his religion, but rather for defaming Islam, revealing secrets and exposing security issues of the Muslims. However, during the conquest of Mecca, the Prophet pardoned him.

31. Is Imam Ali (a) considered a *sayed*?

Imam Ali (a) is considered to be a *sayed* because the definition of a *sayed* is a male who traces his lineage through the paternal line to Hashim, who was Prophet Muhammad's (ṣ) great-grandfather. Prophet Muhammad's (ṣ) father and Imam Ali's (a) father were brothers, so they both trace their lineage through their fathers to Hashim. A female who traces her paternal lineage to Hashim is called a *sayeda*.

In Iran and Iraq, the term *sayed* is typically used, while in countries like Saudi Arabia and Jordan, the term is *sharif* is used although it has the same meaning.

The majority of *sayeds* today are the descendants of Prophet Muhammad (ṣ) through his daughter Fatima (a) and his cousin Imam Ali (a). In many Muslim societies, *sayeds* are shown greater respect and are given a special status not because they are better than others or superior to them in any way. The greater respect that is given to them is essentially being given to the Prophet, as they are his descendants. In many cultures around the world, one way in which people express their respect to a prominent individual is by respecting his children and family.

Furthermore, *sayeds* are permitted use of *khums*, the one-fifth tax, because they are not entitled to receive *zakat*, or the obligatory tithe. Every *sayed* or *sayeda* is entitled to *khums* if he or she is in need.

32. Why is the Grand Mosque in Mecca referred to as *Masjid al-Haram*?

The word *haram* has two definitions, and both accurately describe the Grand Mosque.

In the first sense, *haram* means "sacred." Indeed, the Grand Mosque is sacred to all human beings, and especially the Muslims.

The second sense of *haram* is "forbidden." Bloodshed and aggression, for example, are forbidden on the grounds of the Grand Mosque. Even if a known criminal enters this Mosque, custodians are not allowed to apprehend him. Sanctions may be placed on that individual to result in his voluntary surrender. The Grand Mosque was meant to be an oasis of peace and tranquility, and even animals should not be harmed in it.

Islamic Beliefs and Practices

33. In submitting to God, we encounter great challenges. Is God testing our faith, or is there something else that He wants to prove?

God promises people that they will be tested. The Noble Qur'an states:

> *Do people think that they will be left alone on saying, 'We believe',*
> *and not be tried? And certainly We tried those before them, so God*
> *will certainly know those who are true and He will certainly know*
> *the liars.*[46]

This verse implies that no one will be exempt from the Divine trials. God tried all of the prophets and His great patrons through different calamities and hardships, and thus everyone will be tried to different degrees. Some people will receive easier tests, and some may face daunting examinations depending on their ability of endurance.

There are a number of reasons why God presents us with difficulties and hardships in this life:

1. First, the more hardships an individual endures and is able to overcome, the greater God's reward will be, and the higher one will spiritually ascend. It has been narrated that on the Day of Judgment when the believers will witness their heavenly reward for enduring worldly hardships, they

---

[46] *Noble Qur'an*, Suratul Ankabut (29), verses 2–3

will wish that they had sacrificed more and gone through more hardships.[47]

2. Secondly, through hardships and difficulties, God cleanses us from our sins, for it is a way of expiating our bad deeds. It is much more in our interest to pay off our sins in this life instead of on the Day of Judgment and beyond. The suffering we experience in this life is nothing compared to the chastisement of the hereafter.

3. Third, sometimes God puts us through difficulties so that we may come to appreciate His blessings. We generally appreciate and value our health once we lose it. Unlike those who live in areas where rainfall is abundant year round, those who live in the desert appreciate every drop of rain that they receive. We take God's blessings for granted, and difficulties and hardships are a way of reminding us that we are engulfed in God's blessings. Therefore, one should not view his challenges as a curse or condemnation from God, but rather a great mercy from Him.

One great prophet, Prophet Zachariah (a), was being chased by people who wanted to kill him.[48] He sought refuge within the cavity of an old tree, and when his pursuers reached the tree, they kept him inside of it and chose to saw through the tree. As they reached Prophet Zachariah's (a) skin with the saw and drew blood, he nearly screamed out in pain when God sent Angel Gabriel (a). The angel warned him that if he screamed, God would remove him

---

[47] *Al-Kafi*, vol. 2, p. 255 (Chapter "*Shiddat Ibtila'a al-Mu'min*", tradition 15)

[48] *Jami' al-Sa'adat*, vol. 3, p. 224

from the list of prophets. Prophet Zachariah (a) was thus martyred but he never screamed - he remained patient as he died.

Few of us will ever be asked to make such a sacrifice, but all Muslims must wholeheartedly accept whatever tests and hardships God presents to them and must do their best to pass them successfully.

The word *Muslim* means one who submits entirely to the will of God. In times of hardship, when we are not too sure of the proper path, God will decide for us and we just have to follow.

Indeed, the path of devotion and piety is not paved with flowers and red carpets; rather, it may be filled with thorns and mud. However, the difficult path eventually leads to a great oasis of peace. As the saying goes, the tree of patience is sour, but its fruits are sweet.

34. Are all of the prophets equal? If so, why is there so much attention paid to Prophet Muhammad (s) during the prayers but not the other prophets?

There is no doubt that the prophets are not all equal in their status in the eyes of God. The Qur'an says:

> *We have made some of these messengers to excel the others, among them are they to whom God spoke, and some of them He exalted by (many degrees of) rank; and We gave clear miracles to Jesus son of Mary, and strengthened him with the holy spirit.*[49]

---

[49] *Noble Qur'an*, Suratul Baqarah (2), verse 253

Obviously, favoring one prophet over another is due to the superior nature of the one favored. God does not favor one prophet over another without a valid reason.

All Muslims agree that five prophets stand above all of the others, and they are: Noah (a), Abraham (a), Moses (a), Jesus (a), and Muhammad (ṣ). They are called *Ulul Azm*, or "the prophets with strong determination." Even though Prophet Adam (a) was God's first representative on the earth, he is not among them. In regards to him, God said: "And certainly We gave a commandment to Adam before, but he forgot; and We did not find in him determination."[50]

Even though we Muslims do not regard all of the prophets as having the same stature, at the same time, we do not reject the authority of any of the prophets. We accept all of the prophets of God, following the injunction which has been mentioned in the Qur'an:

> *The messenger believes in what has been revealed to him from his Lord, and (so do) the believers; they all believe in God and His angels and His books and His messengers; We make no difference between any of His messengers; and they say: We hear and we obey, our Lord! Your forgiveness (do we seek), and to You is the eventual course (of return).*[51]

Unlike the Jews who recognize the messages of certain prophets, but reject the message of Prophet Jesus (a); and unlike the Christians, who recognize the messages of Prophet Jesus (a) and all

---

[50] *Noble Qur'an*, Surat Taha (20), verse 115

[51] *Noble Qur'an*, Suratul Baqarah (2), verse 285

of the Jewish prophets, but do not recognize the message of Prophet Muhammad (ṣ), Muslims accept the message of all of the prophets. Muslims believe that God elevated Prophet Muhammad (ṣ) over all of the others. The Qur'an indicates that God gives the utmost respect, love, and compassion to His most beloved messenger – Prophet Muhammad (ṣ).

For example, in many verses of the Qur'an, God addresses all of the prophets by their first names:

And We called out to him saying: O Abraham! You have indeed shown the truth of the vision; surely thus do We reward the doers of good.[52]

And what is this in your right hand, O Moses![53]

O John! Take hold of the Book with strength, and We granted him wisdom while yet a child[54]

And when God said: O Jesus, I am going to terminate the period of your stay (on earth) and cause you to ascend unto Me and purify you from those who disbelieve and make those who follow you above those who disbelieve to the day of resurrection; then to Me shall be your return, so I will decide between you concerning that in which you differed.[55]

---

[52] *Noble Qur'an*, Suratul Saffaat (37) verses 104–105

[53] *Noble Qur'an*, Surat Taha (20), verse 17

[54] *Noble Qur'an*, Surat Maryam (19), verse 12

[55] *Noble Qur'an*, Surat Aale Imran (3), verse 55

And (We said): O Adam! Dwell you and your wife in the garden; so eat from where you desire, but do not go near this tree, for then you will be of the unjust.[56]

However, not once in the entire Qur'an, the actual word of God, does He address Prophet Muhammad (ṣ) by his first name. In every case He addresses the Prophet by his honorific titles: "O you the Prophet" or "O you the Messenger."

While Prophet Muhammad (ṣ) is superior to all of the other prophets in terms of his personal virtues and status, all prophets are equal in terms of the significance of their message and their representation of God on the earth. Greater attention is also given to Prophet Muhammad (ṣ) because he is the seal of all of the prophets and his teachings encapsulate the teachings of all of the other prophets. In addition, he achieved the highest standards of completion and perfection. He is, indeed, God's greatest creation.

35. Why do Muslims mention Prophet Muhammad (s) in their prayers, but not the other prophets?

Muslims mention Prophet Muhammad (ṣ) in their prayers because God says in the Qur'an: "Surely God and His angels send prayers upon the Prophet; O you who believe! Call for (Divine) blessings on him and salute him with a (becoming) salutation."[57]

When God sends His prayers on Prophet Muhammad (ṣ), it means that God raises his status to make the Prophet "closer" to Him. When Muslims send their prayers on the Prophet, it means they are *asking* God to raise the status of the Prophet so that he

---

[56] *Noble Qur'an*, Suratul A'raf (7), verse 19

[57] *Noble Qur'an*, Suratul Ahzab (33), verse 56

may be "closer' to Him. In return, the Prophet will intercede on our behalf and ask God to raise our status, forgive us, and grant us paradise.

The most common way to salute the Prophet and evoke blessings upon him is to say: "*Allahumma salli ala Muhammad wa aale Muhammad*," and this means: "O God, send your blessings upon Muhammad and the family of Muhammad."

Of course, it is highly recommended to mention some of the other prophets, such as Prophet Abraham (a), after sending prayers on Prophet Muhammad (ṣ) and his family, but it is not mandatory. The validity of one's prayer is not contingent upon mentioning other prophets, but Muslim scholars state that if one does not send prayers upon Prophet Muhammad (ṣ) and his family in one's prayer (in the recitation while sitting after prostration), the prayer is invalid.

In fact, al-Shafi'i, who was the leader of the Sunni Shafi'i school of thought, says in one of his poems praising the Ahlul Bayt:

O you family of the Messenger of God,

Your love is an obligation prescribed by Allah in the Qur'an which He revealed.

It is enough for your great status that,

Whoever does not pray for you has no prayer [his prayer is of no worth].[58]

---

[58] *Al-Sawa'iq al-Muhriqa*, p. 88

36. What is infallibility?

Infallibility, simply put, is a universally correct, decision-making process and behavior which is enacted by not only Prophet Muhammad (ṣ), but also by all previous prophets such as Prophets Jesus (a) and Abraham (a). Shia Muslims also add Fatima (a), the daughter of the Prophet, and the twelve revered Imams who are the Divinely inspired direct descendants of Prophet Muhammad (ṣ) into the list of individuals who have been given this special honour and designation.

Different religions have different ideas about the nature of infallibility and its scope. Catholicism, for example, defines papal infallibility somewhat narrowly - for the Pope it applies to matters of Divine revelation, but not to everyday communication or conduct. In Islam, infallibility extends to any sin, iniquity, or indecency—public or private—in addition to religious rulings.

To be clear, being infallible does *not* mean that the Prophets or Imams were not capable of committing sins or speaking untruthfully; rather, their infallibility stems from their piety and profound knowledge of God's laws. Their love of God was so deep that they would never risk challenging Him by committing even the smallest of sins. They also did not commit sins because they vividly understood how ugly it was to commit them. All sins are harmful to us, and they had the insight to realize this harm. Thus, their infallibility came through intention and self-restraint as much as it came from inherent perfection.

The average human being also possesses a certain level of infallibility, for there are certain acts which we would not perform in public. A small child, however, may not find a barrier holding him from committing that same action. Being adults, we see the ugliness of certain actions that a child may not see.

As the religious authorities of the Muslim community, Prophet Muhammad (ṣ) and the Imams were appointed by God to lead the people and teach them moral principles. They accepted a sacred duty from God not to commit any sins. Otherwise, that would have contradicted their reason for being sent. If a prophet would have sinned then it would have implied that God legitimized sinning as God orders all people to follow the prophets, and therefore God gives legitimacy to all of the acts of the prophets. From the Qur'an we read the following verse:

> And We did not send any messenger but that he should be obeyed by God's permission; and had they, when they were unjust to themselves, come to you and asked forgiveness from God and the Messenger had (also) asked forgiveness for them, they would have found God Oft-returning (to mercy), Merciful. But no! By your Lord! They will not believe (in your message) until they make you a judge of that which has become a matter of disagreement among them, and then do not find any straightness in their hearts as to what you have decided and submit with entire submission.[59]

37. If the twelve Imams are infallible, then why did they often speak about God forgiving their sins?

The answer has two parts:

First of all, the Imams, being educators, tutors, and leaders, functioned as conduits between God and the people (not just

---

[59] *Noble Qur'an*, Suratul Nisa (4), verses 64–65

Muslims but rather, for all of humanity). They are the ones who taught mankind how to worship God properly. When they spoke about their "sins," they were actually speaking about the sins of the average person. This was a symbolic gesture meant to educate people, similar to a father teaching his son how to perform the daily prayers.

The other part of this answer lies in the strict standards that the Imams held for themselves. The Imams, whose lives were dominated by the love of God, always felt they had shortcomings towards their duties to God. Although they never had any shortcomings and had achieved the highest possible ranks of obedience to God, they would implore God for His forgiveness. They would frequently weep and grieve to express their utter humbleness and humility towards God and their unparalleled love for Him. They demonstrated how they were true slaves of God and how only He was the true Master.

The fourth Imam, Ali Zain al-Abideen (a), demonstrated this devotion in one especially harrowing incident. One day, while the Imam was praying, his child fell into a well. The child's caretaker came screaming to tell the Imam that his baby had fallen into the well, but the Imam did not interrupt his prayer to respond to her. The woman said, "What a ruthless heart you, the children of Hashim (meaning the Imams), have!"

The Imam kept on praying as if nothing had happened. When he finished, he went to the well, sat on the edge, and uttered a few words - apparently a prayer to God. The water level in the well started to rise and the Imam stretched out his hand and recovered his son, who was still alive. He then gave him to the caretaker and said: "Take this baby, O you with weak faith," and added: "Don't you know that I was standing before the Lord of heavens and the Lord of the earth, and if I would have turned my face a bit away from Him, He then would have definitely turned His face from me!?"[60]

It is important to note here that one must achieve an extremely high level of faith and closeness to God to respond the way that the Imam did. For those of us who do not possess such a great status with God, our primary obligation would be to save the life of a child that is in jeopardy.

38. What is the relationship between the return of the twelfth Imam and the Day of Judgment?

A narration from Prophet Muhammad (ṣ) says: "If there remains only one day before the Day of Judgment, God will prolong that day until a man from my progeny will appear. He will fill the world with justice, just as it had been filled with injustice and aggression."[61] This narration indicates that the advent of Imam al-Mahdi (a) will be sometime before the Day of Judgment; and no one except for God knows exactly when this will be. The Noble Qur'an states:

They ask you about the hour, when will be its taking place? Say:
The knowledge of it is only with my Lord; none but He shall
manifest it at its time; it will be momentous in the heavens and the
earth; it will not come upon you but all of a sudden. They ask you

---

[60] *Al-Thaqib fil manaqib*, p. 149

[61] *Al-Ghayba* of al-Tusi, p. 180

as if you were solicitous about it. Say: Its knowledge is only with God, but most people do not know.[62]

The appearance of the twelfth Imam shall precede the Day of Judgment and will signal that the end of the earthly world is coming near.

Some narrations say that Imam al-Mahdi (a) will rule for seven or nineteen years, but these narrations point out that the span of those years will differ from our years of 365 days - those years will be much longer. Some narrations also mention that at the end of his rule, the Imam will be murdered. During the time of his rule, however long it may be, he will establish law and justice, and that is what is really important.

39. What is *taqleed*?

Taqleed means referring to a scholar in his edicts and verdicts and applying them in our day to day life. This is similar to a sick person seeking treatment from a physician, or an individual who wants to build a skyscraper consulting an architect.

It is binding for Muslims who are not scholars in Islamic jurisprudence to follow a scholar (a *mujtahid*) who has reached the highest level of ability to derive Islamic laws from original and authentic Islamic sources (a process called *ijtihad* or deducing the legal laws of the Islamic faith through referencing the four primary sources – the Qur'an, the hadith, the intellect and the consensus of the past jurists).

---

[62] *Noble Qur'an*, Suratul A'raf (7), verse 187

Becoming capable of exercising *ijtihad* is extremely complex and requires decades of study of the Arabic language, Arabic grammar and eloquence, comprehension of the Qur'an, Islamic jurisprudence, and the principles of Islamic jurisprudence. It also requires a grasp of contemporary fields of knowledge such as psychology, sociology, history, world religions, philosophy, and logic.

It is incumbent upon Muslims who are not scholars not only to seek a *mujtahid's* opinion and apply it - but also to verify that the scholar is deemed the most knowledgeable individual in the field of Islam.

40. What conditions permit a Muslim to switch *taqleed* from one scholar to another?

A Muslim may switch if the scholar his is following dies or if he discovers (through personal research or the testimony of reliable scholars) that another scholar is more knowledgeable in jurisprudence.

If a Muslim's chosen scholar dies, then he must switch to the most knowledgeable living scholar, or he may continue following his deceased mujtahid's opinions only with the permission of the most knowledgeable living scholar. Also, Muslims may change their *taqleed* if their current scholar becomes incapacitated, such as by a stroke or loss of mind.

41. What is *barzakh*, and what can we expect there?

Barzakh, literally translated, is a distance between two areas - whether it is a partition or an interval of time. In terms of after death, it refers to the area or time interval that separates this world from the Day of Judgment. The Noble Qur'an stats:

> Until when death overtakes one of them, he says: Send me back, my
> Lord, send me back; Haply I may do good in that which I have left.
> By no means! it is a (mere) word that he speaks; and before them is
> a barrier (barzakh) until the day they are raised.[63]

Upon departure from this life, people's souls will be taken into *barzakh*. In one narration, Prophet Muhammad (ṣ) said: "The grave is either a garden of paradise or a pit of hellfire."[64] From this, we understand that every person will either be punished or rewarded in the grave during the *barzakh* period.

Imam Muhammad al-Jawad (a), the ninth Imam, compared what happens in *barzakh* to what happens in our dreams: there are nightmares for some people and pleasant dreams for others. The reward or punishment will not be directed at the physical human body, but rather upon the soul. Accounts narrated by the Imams say that the souls of the righteous people in *barzakh* will be together, and they will enjoy the abundant rewards of God, the Almighty.

Christians contemplating *barzakh* might see resemblances to purgatory. With respect to those people who are destined to heaven but they committed some sins in this life, the two religions are similar in that they both state the souls will be punished temporarily to expiate their sins before being admitted to heaven.

---

[63] *Noble Qur'an*, Suratul Mu'minoon (23), verses 99–100
[64] *Al-Amaali* of al-Sadooq, p. 28

There are several differences, however. In *barzakh*, those who are destined for heaven will not enter it until the Day of Judgment. They will enjoy heaven-like rewards in *barzakh*, but the actual rewards of heaven will only be given to them when they enter heaven after the Day of Judgment. The second difference is that all of the souls must pass through *barzakh*, even those who are destined to hell. The third difference is that not all of the souls will be punished in *barzakh*. Hence, there are four groups of people who will have different experiences:

1. The first group will enter heaven without being punished at all, for they are the most righteous of people. In *barzakh*, God will bestow them with heaven-like rewards.

2. The second group will also enter heaven, but only after being punished for the sins that they committed. Then they will be rewarded for the good deeds that they offered in this life.

3. The third group will be punished both in *barzakh* and in hell, but after expiating their sins in hell they will be forgiven and taken to heaven.

4. The fourth group, which is the most miserable, will be punished in *barzakh* and in hell, and they will remain in the hell-fire. An example of this group are those evil people who willfully perpetrated heinous crimes, such as the mass-murders, those who enacted genocide against humanity, or those who killed the Prophets and Imams and never truly repented in their lives.

42. Will God's "throne" be visible in the hereafter?

In Islam, references to the throne of God evoke the power and majesty of the Divine, just as they do in Judaism and Christianity. In Christianity, some descriptions of the throne appear to be figurative, while Jewish scholars have pointed out the symbolic nature of literal-sounding passages about God's throne-chariot. Islamic scholars, by contrast, are quite open about the throne existing as a physical object.

The Qur'an mentions the throne at least twenty-two times, here in a verse about the Day of Judgment, when eight great angels will carry the throne while shading the Prophets, Imams, and selected righteous:

> And the angels shall be on the sides thereof; and above them eight shall bear on that day your Lord's throne.[67]

Interestingly, the New Testament states that seven Spirits surround the throne.[68]

Another verse in the Noble Qur'an states:

> He it is Who created the heavens and the earth in six Days—and His throne was over the water—that He might try you, which of you is best in conduct. But if you (Muhammad) were to say to them, "You shall indeed be raised up after death," the unbelievers would be sure to say, "This is nothing but obvious sorcery!"[69]

---

[67] Noble Qur'an, Suratul Haqqah (69), verse 17
[68] Bible, Book of Revelation, 1:4
[69] Noble Qur'an, Surat Hud (11), verse 7

However, it is highly important to note that the existence of a physical throne does not imply in any way that God is corporeal or has human qualities. God does not sit upon a throne the way a human king would simply because He has no physical body. No throne can contain God's glorified presence.

Islamic narrations tell us that the throne is one of God's greatest creations, and the entire universe is surrounded by the throne of God. Hence, God's physical throne symbolizes His absolute power and control over the universe.

Some Qur'anic commentators take the word "throne" as a metonymy for the power of God, since a throne is the physical manifestation of any king's real power. They believe there might not be a physical throne.

Whether we believe there is a physical throne or not, we should not have the illusion of seeing God sitting on the throne as a king would, and the important idea here is that the Almighty God commands absolute control over the entire universe.

43. How can one distinguish between miracles of prophethood and illusions?

Illusions are ephemeral and can be exposed, if not by ordinary people then by magicians who know their secrets. Miracles, on the other hand, are immutable and indomitable.

This concept was best demonstrated when Prophet Moses (a) showed Pharaoh his miracle: God turned his cane into a snake. This prompted Pharaoh, who presumed that it was a form of magic, to summon all of the sorcerers in Egypt to defeat the alleged magic.

When 600 sorcerers gathered to battle Prophet Moses (a) and turned their staffs into what appeared as snakes, the staff of Prophet Moses (a) turned into a real snake and swallowed all of their staffs. This proved that his miracle was not an illusion. Pharaoh's sorcerers, who realized this, were the first among the believers, and they declared before Pharaoh their beliefs and submitted to the Lord of Moses (a). Pharaoh became angry at their confessions and threatened to cut off their hands and feet and crucify all of them on trees. But of course none of his intimidation and threats worked, for the sorcerers had become steadfast on the path of God.

A miracle, therefore, can only be performed by a representative of God, and it cannot be reproduced or countered by anyone else.

44. What is the significance of bowing (*ruku*) in prayer?

Imam Ali (a) offers a very beautiful interpretation of the gestures of prayer, including bowing. He says that when a person says "God is the greatest" (known as the *takbir*), marking the beginning of the prayer, and brings his two hands parallel to his ears, it symbolizes disconnection from the outer world and complete engagement with God. It is as if one is putting everything behind him and is focusing only on God. Standing during prayer while reciting the Qur'an resembles how all of humankind will stand before God on the Day of Judgment.

Bowing (*ruku*) is a gesture in which a Muslim symbolizes a victim's act of submission to his executioner. So during the act of bowing, we are displaying our absolute humbleness and submission to God. The two prostrations (*sujood*), according to

Imam Ali (a), symbolize the concepts of life, death, and resurrection.

Imam Ali (a) says the first prostration indicates the origin from which the human being is made, meaning the earth. Raising one's head symbolizes our creation from earth and our journey into this worldly life. Going to the second prostration symbolizes our death when we will return back to our mother earth. Raising one's head again from the second prostration symbolizes the resurrection on the Day of Judgment.

Indeed, all gestures during prayer are "silent," yet speak eloquently about the fact that we are all God's creations and subject to His ultimate decree. We demonstrate these great values with God both verbally and physically throughout the actions in our prayers.

45. Why do some Muslims pray with their hands folded?

In Sahih al-Bukhari, the most authentic Sunni book of sayings of Prophet Muhammad (ṣ), there is a narration in the "The Book of Prayers" in the chapter titled "The Characteristics of Prayer." In it, one companion of the Prophet says, "We have been ordered to fold our hands in prayer."[70] The narrator does not directly say that the Prophet gave this order, nor does he specify anyone else.

The narrator, Abu Hazim, implies that folding one's hands is mandatory and gives the impression that the Prophet ordered it. In fact, Prophet Muhammad (ṣ) never ordered Muslims to fold

---

[70] *Sahih al-Bukhari*, vol. 1, book 12, hadith 707: Narrated Sahl bin Sa'd: "The people were ordered to place the right hand on the left forearm in the prayer. Abu Hazim said: I knew that the order was from the Prophet."

their hands while praying. It was the second Caliph, Omar ibn al-Khattab, who ordered this act to be inserted in the prayer during his rule as the Caliph.

According to authentic historical accounts, the Prophet never prayed with his hands folded. The same was true for the first Caliph, Abu Bakr. This practice started during Omar's time as the Caliph, when the Muslims conquered Persia in the year 17 AH.

Persian war prisoners were brought to Medina, the capital of Islam, to be displayed before Omar. Ancient Persians were known for highly respecting their emperors and monarchs. When the Persian war prisoners were brought to the mosque where Omar was seated, they folded their hands on their chests out of respect. Omar was amazed and impressed by this gesture, and he said that if this gesture is for respect, then God deserves this mode of respect, and he ordered the Muslims to fold their hands while praying.[71]

It must be kept in mind that no one—not even Prophet Muhammad (s)—has the right to add anything to the prayers that have been prescribed by God. Therefore, many Muslims today, such as the Shia and the Malikis (one of the sects within the Sunni faith), do not fold their hands in prayer because the Prophet simply did not do so.

---

[71] *Mustanad al-Urwa al-Wuthqa*, vol. 4, pp. 445–446; *Jawaher al-Kalam*, vol. 11, p. 19

46. Prophet Muhammad (s) occasionally combined his daily prayers. How do Shia Muslims justify combining their prayers every day?

The Shia conclude from the Prophet's act of combining of prayers that combining prayers is in fact a choice and is allowed in all instances.

As found in *Sahih al-Bukhari* (narrated by Ibn Abbas):

The Prophet prayed seven rak'at together (Maghrib and Isha) and eight rak'at (Dhuhr and Asr) together [during one time interval rather than having a large time separation between the prayers].[72]

In addition, it has been narrated in *Sahih al-Muslim* that:

Ibn Abbas reported: The Messenger of Allah (may peace be upon him) observed the noon and afternoon prayers together in Medina without being in a state of fear or in a state of journey. (Abu Zubair said: I asked Sa'id [one of the narrators] why he did that. He said: I asked Ibn Abbas as you have asked me, and he replied that he [the Prophet] wanted that no one among his nation should be put to [unnecessary] hardship.)[73]

In this day and age, when people are working longer hours, it is definitely an advantage to combine the prayers where it is allowed. Since combining the two prayers is more convenient to most people and requires less effort to prepare for, the Shia take advantage of this gift from God and combine their prayers.

---

[72] *Sahih al-Bukhari*, vol. 1, book 10, hadith 537
[73] *Sahih Muslim*, book 4 (The Book of Prayers), ch. 99, hadith 1516

Let us not forget the verse in the Qur'an where God says that He has not imposed upon us any hardship beyond the extent of our ability to bear:

And (as for) those who believe and do good We do not impose on any soul a duty except to the extent of its ability - they are the dwellers of the garden; in it they shall abide.[74]

It can be hard on certain Muslims who have busy schedules to separate their prayers. Therefore, combining the noon and afternoon prayers, and the evening and night prayers is permissible. Even so, Shia Muslims do not deny that separating the prayers is also permissible.

Combining the prayers, therefore, is not mandatory; nor is it mandatory to separate them. It is a matter of choice, and we are free to combine our prayers or separate them.

Some scholars say that it is better to combine them, while others have stated that it is better to separate them. Those scholars who state that it is better to combine them say that the Qur'an highly encourages us to hasten toward the mercy of God. Certainly, prayer is one of the greatest manifestations of God's mercy.

And hasten to forgiveness from your Lord; and a Garden, the extensiveness of which is (as) the heavens and the earth, it is prepared for those who guard (against evil).[75]

---

[74] *Noble Qur'an*, Suratul A'raf (7), verse 42
[75] *Noble Qur'an*, Suratul Aale Imran (3), verse 133

Some Sunni scholars have said that the Prophet used to combine his prayers only in times of hardship and fear. However there are authentic Sunni narrations, such as the ones stated previously from Sahih al-Bukhari and Sahih Muslim that state the Prophet sometimes combined the prayers without any hardship or fear. This proves that one is free to choose whether to separate or combine one's prayers.

According to many scholars, separating between the prayers does not mean that one must wait two or three hours before performing the following prayer. Separation between the two prayers occurs by the mere performance of the *ta'qeebat* - the recommended supplications following the prayers, such as saying God is Greatest (*Allahu Akbar*). Other recommended supplications include the recitation of *Tasbeehat al-Zahra*, which is to pronounce thirty-four times God is Greatest (*Allahu Akbar)*, thirty-three times Glory be to God (*Subhanallah*), and thirty-three times Praise be to God (*Al-Hamdulillah*). This prayer is a gift that Prophet Muhammad (ṣ) gave to his daughter Fatima al-Zahra (a). Therefore, even those who are believed to combine their prayers actually do separate them - just with a shorter time between them.

What is necessary to point out is that it is not really the prayers that are being combined, but the prayer times. In other words, combining the noon (*dhuhr*) and afternoon (*asr*) prayers does not result in one prayer of eight units. After the noon prayer, there is only a very short break before the time for the afternoon prayer. This break may constitute saying God is Greatest three times, or it may take enough time to recite *Tasbeehat al-Zahra* or the extra recommended supplications of a given prayer. Regardless, the time for the afternoon prayer commences immediately after the completion of the noon prayer; and the same holds true for the evening prayers.

Interestingly, the Qur'an indicates that the major prayer times are three: noon, dusk, and dawn, in the following verse:

Keep up the prayer from the declining of the sun (noon), until the darkness of the night (after sunset), and the morning recitation (fajr); surely the morning recitation is witnessed.[76]

And keep up the prayer in the two parts of the day and in the first hours of the night; surely good deeds take away evil deeds; this is a reminder to the mindful.[77]

These verses illustrate that the times for the other two prayers, the afternoon and night prayers, are secondary times to the three major times: noon, dusk, and dawn. Therefore, one can conclude that the Qur'an also indirectly permits Muslims to combine their noon and afternoon prayers as well as their evening and night prayers.

47. If Prophet Muhammad (s) did not pray on prayer tablets from Karbala, then why do Shia Muslims do it?

The immaculate Imams of the Ahlul Bayt are mere relators of the statements and sayings of Prophet Muhammad (ṣ). The content of their narrations comes from Prophet Muhammad (ṣ), and the Prophet's speech comes from God Almighty.

---

[76] *Noble Qur'an*, Suratul Isra (17), verse 78
[77] *Noble Qur'an*, Surat Hud (11), verse 114

Our Imams have taught us that it is highly recommended to prostrate on the soil of Imam al-Husayn's (a) burial site in Karbala. One narration by Imam al-Sadiq (a) states that "prostrating on the soil (*turbah*) of Imam al-Husayn (a) (during prayer) will penetrate the seven barriers to heaven, and the prayer will thus be accepted."[78] Indeed, this is a gift that God has rewarded Imam al-Husayn (a) with for his great sacrifices—sacrifices which are unparalleled in the annals of history.

Obviously, the Prophet was not alive at the time of the tragedy of Karbala, so he could not pray on that soil. However, the Prophet, knowing about his grandson's great martyrdom, foretold of that tragic event and passed on this knowledge to his heirs and successors, the infallible Imams of the Ahlul Bayt. Had the Prophet been able to pray on the soil from Karbala, then he certainly would have. It is he who instructed the infallible Imams to issue such a narration revering the soil of Karbala, where Imam al-Husayn (a) was martyred.

However, praying on the clay tablet made from that sacred soil is only highly recommended, and a Muslim is not obliged to prostrate on it. One's prayer is valid if he prostrates on any ground or piece of earth.

48. Why do Shia Muslims place their hands on their heads when they mention Imam al-Mahdi (a)?

We do so as a sign of reverence and respect for Imam al-Mahdi (a), the awaited savior, because he is alive and is the Imam of our time. It is a salutation, a symbol of support, and a sign of respect to him.

---

[78] *Wasael al-Shia*, vol. 5, p. 366

It has been narrated that when a poet mentioned Imam al-Mahdi (a) in the presence of Imam al-Redha (a), the Imam stood and placed his hand on his head. [79]

Some scholars believe this gesture is a reference to the intellectual completion that people will experience when Imam al-Mahdi (a) will reappear. He will present the pristine teachings of God such that everyone in the world will embrace them, thereby increasing their intellectual capacity.

49. Why is the black stone (In Mecca) such an important object in Islam?

According to some narrations, Angel Gabriel brought down the black stone from heaven to Prophet Adam (a) when he first built the Ka'bah, the sacred cube-shaped building in Mecca now at the center of the Grand Mosque. [80] These narrations say that the black stone was a gem in paradise, while other narrations state that it was an angel. It is possible that the gem is always accompanied by an angel. The stone used to be transparent. One narration says it was whiter than milk and more luminous than the sun, but it was blackened by the sins of people. [81]

When Prophet Abraham (a) later rebuilt the Ka'bah, God instructed him to mount the black stone on one of the corners of the Ka'bah. [82] The purpose of the black stone is to remind us of our

---

[79] *Mustadrak Safeenat al-Bihar*, vol. 8, p. 629

[80] *Al-Kafi*, vol. 4, p. 185 and *Bihar al-Anwar*, vol. 81, p. 77–78

[81] *Al-Kafi*, vol. 4, p. 191

[82] *Al-Kafi*, vol. 4, p. 205

covenant with God. The Qur'an tells us that before we came into this life, a covenant took place between us and God:

> And when your Lord brought forth from the children of Adam, from their backs, their descendants, and made them bear witness against their own souls: Am I not your Lord? They said: Yes! we bear witness. Lest you should say on the day of resurrection: Surely we were heedless of this. [83]

Narrations tell us that this covenant took place where the black stone now sits. [84] Muslims who visit the Grand Mosque in Mecca and pass by the black stone are recommended to remind themselves of that covenant and be determined to uphold it by keeping their faith in God and practicing His teachings. Prophet Muhammad (ṣ) used to kiss the black stone,[85] and that is why many Muslims even today continue to kiss the black stone when they visit the Grand Mosque in Mecca.

50. Is music prohibited in Islam?

Scholars of Islam have two opinions about music.

The first group of scholars deems all music as satanic mediums and potentially so distracting that it may keep the minds of Muslims away from God and the hereafter. For this group of scholars, all types of music are prohibited (*haram*), and they advise their followers to completely stay away from music. There is some scientific evidence that confirms the negative impacts of music on

---

[83] *Noble Qur'an*, Suratul A'raf (7), verse 172

[84] *Al-Kafi*, vol. 4, p. 185

[85] *Sahih al-Bukhari*, hadith no. 1520

a person. Some of these negative effects include changes in mood, irregular heartbeats, and problems with digestion. Due to its addictive nature, music sometimes acts like a drug. Prolonged exposure to many types of music often leads to depression. We also have some narrations which state that listening to music can lead to other sins.

The second group of scholars differentiates between two types of music. The first type of music is suggestive and provocative, and it distracts Muslims from their Islamic responsibilities, while awakening in them their instinctual desires. This type of music, such as pop music, is prohibited (*haram*) in the eyes of these scholars. Muslims listening intentionally to these types of music are committing a sin. The second category consists of classical music, music accompanying military marches, pictorial music, and any other music that does not fit in the first category. This type of music is permissible for Muslims according to this group of scholars. Muslims need to check with their own religious authority (*Marja'*) in regards to this issue.

51. At what age should a person write a will?

There is no specific age for a will to be written; however, the writer of the will must be mature and sane. It is recommended that the will be written as early as possible, for there is a *hadith* which says that the act of writing one's will actually prolongs one's life.[86] Also, Prophet Muhammad (ṣ) says: "No Muslim who believes in God and His messenger should sleep, except that his will is beneath his head [when he goes to sleep]." In other words, one

---

[86] *Al-Fatawa al-Muayassara*, p. 335

must write a will and keep it in a place such that if he or she were to die, the will could easily be found.

It is worth mentioning that there is no direct correlation between death and the writing of a will. Someone may not write a will and die soon, and someone may not write a will and not die for another eighty years. However, writing a will definitely invokes God's blessings and could lead to a longer, more prosperous life. Even those who write a will and die soon, they may have died earlier had they not written their will. Similarly, those who do not write a will and live a long life may have lived longer had they written their will.

A will does not have to be written and can even be a verbal agreement. Once a person has a will, one should be aware of the Islamic laws of inheritance. Writing a will is best done by the help or advice of an expert in this field.

Islamic Diet

52. Some Muslims believe that eating meat not slaughtered in proper Islamic way is *halal* as long as one mentions the name of God on the meat before eating it. They base this on the verse that says, "And do not eat of that on which God's name has not been mentioned." What is the proper explanation for this verse which can be used to refute their beliefs?

God states in the Qur'an:

> *Forbidden to you is that which dies of itself, and blood, and flesh of swine, and that on which any name other than that of God has been invoked, and the strangled (animal) and that beaten to death, and that killed by a fall and that killed by being smitten with the horn, and that which wild beasts have eaten, except what you slaughter, and what is sacrificed on stones set up (for idols)...but whoever is compelled by hunger, not inclining willfully to sin, then surely God is Forgiving, Merciful.*[87]

Scholars of Islam say that the word *maytah*, as used in the Qur'an, means any animal that is not slaughtered in a way that meets Islamic criteria. Five conditions must be met in order for meat to be considered permissible (*halal*):

1. The butcher (who slaughters the animal) must be Muslim.

2. The animal should be slaughtered facing the direction of the Ka'bah in Mecca.

---

[87] *Noble Qur'an, Suratul Ma'idah (5), verse 3*

3. A sharp knife must be used.

4. The butcher must recite the name of God while slaughtering the animal.

5. The four main veins should be severed.[88]

It is also highly recommended to give the animal some water before slaughtering it, to tie its feet, and to be very careful in slaughtering the animal in a manner that is least painful. Any animal that has not been slaughtered in this manner is deemed *maytah*.

Thus, only mentioning the name of God on the meat before eating it does not make it halal. In fact, God specifically prohibits Muslims from eating meat on which the name of God has not been mentioned at the time of slaughter:

Therefore eat of that on which God's name has been mentioned if you are believers in His communications.[89]

And do not eat of that on which God's name has not been mentioned, and that is most surely a transgression;[90]

The mentioning of God's name over the meat was revealed in the **past** tense in the Qur'an, which means that mentioning God's name must be done *before,* at the time of slaughtering the animal, not at the time of eating it. Therefore, mentioning the name of God over the meat only at the time of eating does not fulfill the Islamic

---

[88] What is meant by the four main veins are the two jugular veins and the two carotid arteries.

[89] *Noble Qu'ran*, Suratul An'aam (6), verse 118

[90] *Noble Qur'an*, Suratul An'aam (6), verse 121

requirements, and consequently, it is prohibited to eat this kind of meat.

53. Some Muslims say that it is okay to eat meat that is slaughtered by Jews and Christians, citing a verse in the Qur'an which permits Muslims to eat the food of the People of the Book. Is this permissible or not?

God says in the Qur'an:

> This day (all of) the good things are allowed to you; and the food (ta'am) of those who have been given the Book is lawful for you and your food is lawful for them.[91]

In this verse, God permits Muslims to eat the "food" offered by non-Muslims. However, the word "food" here does not include all types of food such as pork, or meat that has not been slaughtered in the proper Islamic way.

First of all, this verse uses the Arabic word *ta'am* to refer to the food of non-Muslims. Arabic linguists such as Ibn Mandhour state that during those days the word *ta'am* primarily referred to wheat, barley and dates.[92] Although the word can also include other types of food such as meat, but if someone wanted to refer to other foods using this word, then one would generally also state those foods in specific. Therefore, the verse does not specifically state that the meats of non-Muslims are lawful.

Second, we have narrations from our Imams that explain the meaning of the word *ta'am* used in this verse. Imam al-Sadiq (a)

---

[91] *Noble Qur'an*, Suratul Ma'idah (5), verse 5
[92] *Lisan al-Arab*, under the word "Ta'am."

says that the word *ta'am* here only refers to grains and fruits, and it does not include meats. [93]

Third, other verses in the Qur'an are clear that pork and meat which have not been prepared in the proper Islamic way are forbidden for Muslims to eat. In verse 3 of the same chapter, God says:

> Forbidden to you is that which dies of itself, and blood, and flesh of swine, and that on which any other name than that of God has been invoked, and the strangled (animal) and that beaten to death, and that killed by a fall and that killed by being smitten with the horn, and that which wild beasts have eaten, except what you slaughter, and what is sacrificed on stones set up (for idols) and that you divide by the arrows; that is a transgression. [94]

Thus, we notice in this particular verse that God has prohibited pork and *maytah*. *Maytah* is any animal that dies by itself or an animal that was not slaughtered in the Islamic way. So when we reconcile verses 3 and 5 of the same chapter, and keep in mind that the word *ta'am* primarily referred to grains, then we realize that what is meant by the food of the People of the Book is any food other than pork and animals that are not slaughtered according to Islamic law.

54. Why can Muslims eat only fish that have scales?

When God orders us to do something or refrain from something, we are obligated to show our obedience to Him, for He knows what

---

[93] *Tafsir al-Qummi*, vol. 1, p. 163

[94] *Noble Qur'an*, Suratul Ma'idah (5), verse 3

is best for us. Whether we know the reason behind a specific ruling or not, we still have to follow it. God knows all things better than we do. He may hide the real reason behind a prohibition, but we are still obligated to obey His commands.

Sometimes the real reason may just be to test us, because God asks certain things of people as a test, and we all have to follow. Muslim scholars debate whether there is a real reason for every command given or whether it could just be a test for humanity. The majority of Shia Muslim scholars believe that there are real reasons behind all of God's rulings and commands. The Prophet Muhammad (ṣ) said:

> O people! You are like patients and God is the physician. What is good for the patient rests in what the physician prescribes, not in what the patient desires.[95]

For seafood, the real reason could be what the scientific findings now prove: that some of the Islamically-prohibited fish are bottom feeders. They eat the waste in oceans or lakes, and by doing so, they maintain the equilibrium of marine life. But the substances that they eat could be unhealthy or dangerous for humans to consume.

The criterion for a fish to be permissible (halal) is for it to have scales. Scales provide fish with a protective covering that prevents harmful substances from affecting their body, so fish without scales are more vulnerable to contracting certain diseases. The only permissible seafood that does not fit this criterion is shrimp, as it is halal to eat. Unlike lobsters and crayfish, shrimp are

---

[95] *Mustadrak al-Wasa'el*, vol. 3, p. 177

swimmers rather than crawlers. They are highly nutritious and low in fat and calories.

Another possible reason for prohibition is that some marine creatures such as whales and sharks live on certain other fish (which are not *halal)* in the ocean. Allowing human beings to eat them may in the long run threaten the survival of many of these species.

55. Is gelatin considered lawful (*halal*)?

The ruling for gelatin depends on the source from which it is extracted. If gelatin is extracted from vegetables, then it is permissible (*halal*) to consume, and also if it is extracted from a permissible-to-eat (*halal*) animal, such as a cow that has been slaughtered in an Islamic way, then it is also permissible to eat. However, if gelatin is derived from pork or from a prohibited (*haram*) source, such as a cow that has not been slaughtered in an Islamic way, then its ruling depends on whether the gelatin goes through total transformation during its processing or not.

If we presume that it does go through total and complete transformation, then it is permissible to consume. But if the gelatin does not go through total transformation during its processing, then it is forbidden to consume. An authoritative chemist should testify to the gelatin's total transformation. If chemists believe that gelatin is not transformed entirely during processing, then it would be forbidden to eat.

Scholars differ in their views depending on which chemists they consult. Based on inquiries with several chemists that I have had, I personally believe that gelatin does not go through complete transformation during processing. Therefore, if the gelatin used in food is extracted from pork or non-permissible animals, then I believe it is not permissible. However, if gelatin is made or extracted from vegetables or permissible-to-eat animals which were slaughtered according to Islamic rulings, then it is permissible to eat it.

According to some scholars,[96] if gelatin does not go through total transformation during its processing, but it is extracted from the bones of an animal (excluding pigs), then it is considered permissible even if these animals were not slaughtered in an Islamic way. These scholars believe that the bones of all animals (excluding pigs and dogs) are considered clean (tahir), and thus they are permissible to consume.

---

[96] Ayatollah Sistani

Islamic Morality and Ethics

56. How does one seek forgiveness for sins? Does a larger sin require a greater level of repentance before God will forgive it?

Repentance has several criteria to be observed by the sinner:

1. Asking God for forgiveness and promising that one will try hard not to repeat that sin. If a person is not determined in his heart to refrain from committing the sin again, then he is not really serious about asking for forgiveness.

2. Being remorseful for the sin that one has committed. No remorse means that the sinner is not repentant. Imam Ali (a) said, "He who asks God for forgiveness for what he has done without being remorseful about it, is like someone who is only fooling himself."

3. If one has committed a sin privately, then one must also repent privately. But if one committed a sin publicly, such as degrading or humiliating someone else, then one must also repent publicly. If you wronged someone in the presence of others, then it will not suffice to invoke God's forgiveness privately. You must apologize and seek forgiveness from the person whom you have wronged in the presence of those same people.

4. One must compensate for those sins committed by doing something good. For example, if you used your mouth to verbally hurt someone or lie, then you must use your mouth in

God's obedience such as reciting the holy Qur'an or saying kind words to people. This is how one may truly compensate for one's sins.

Greater sins require a greater sense of remorse. They require the repentant to show more remorse and feel guiltier for what he or she has done, and one must be more determined to not repeat it in the future. In short, one must do everything possible to avoid committing the sin ever again.

57. What can I do to prevent temptations from taking me away from God?

God has endowed the vulnerable human being, who often stands weak before temptation, with certain tools with which he can use to resist the temptation of the Devil and the evil-inciting soul. There are many words of advice given to the believers by the Prophet and his family to resist temptations. The foremost is to be pious and God conscious. The Qur'an indicates that the Devil has no power over the real servants of God.

> *Surely, as regards to My servants, you have no authority over them except those who follow you of the deviators.*[97]

Therefore, the best advice which we can offer to ourselves and to others is to become pious and be actively aware that God is watching us day and night. Pray on time, avoid engaging in nonsensical conversations, refrain from gossiping, and instead, spend time reading the Qur'an or supplications narrated by the Ahlul Bayt, such as Du'a Kumayl, Du'a Sabah, Munajat of Imam Ali

---

[97] *Noble Qur'an*, Suratul Hijr (15), verse 42

(a), and performing the midnight prayer *(Salat al-Layl)*. These will all help us develop an ability to resist temptations.

Do not forget that God wants us to remember Him always. God told Prophet Moses (a), "Moses, remember me during all times." Moses questioned, "My Lord when I go to the bathroom, I am embarrassed to mention your name." God replied, "Moses, mention my name and remember my name all the time."

Having a direct and consistent relationship with God helps us stay away from those things that displease Him. Once a Bedouin asked Prophet Muhammad (ṣ), "What will keep me close to God?" The Prophet answered, "That what keeps you away from the temptations of this worldly life."

One must truly realize that this world is a temporary stage in one's journey; and it is only a transition from this life to the next. Is it worth it to relinquish that eternal bliss because of some limited temptations? Sooner than we think, we will depart from this life, and we will have to put everything behind us except our good deeds. No matter how much difficulty we endure in this life, sooner than we think it will end one day and be over, but for those people who are faithful, they we will be eternally relieved.

It has been narrated that once Prophet David (a) was reciting the Psalms when he came across Prophet Ezekiel (a) near a mountain. David asked him, "Have you ever thought of committing a sin?" He replied no. Then David asked him, "Have you ever felt attracted to the temptations and cravings of this world?" Ezekiel admitted that his heart sometimes is pulled by the temptations of this life. David then asked him, "So what do you do when you feel enticed?" Ezekiel replied, "I enter this cave." When they entered the cave, he told David to look at a tablet that hung right above a bed which carried the remains of a skeleton on it; and he told him to read the inscription on the tablet. It read, "I am King Arwa the son of Salm. I ruled for one thousand years, built one thousand cities, and owned one thousand female slaves - but this is my end. Soil has become my bed, the rocks have become my pillow, and worms and snakes have become my neighbors. Whoever sees me should not be deceived by this world." Whenever Ezekiel felt tempted by his worldly desires, he simply took a look at the remains of this king. If this is the king's end, despite his vast kingdom, then what about him?[98]

58. Why is intercession necessary if we can directly ask God to forgive us? Who can intercede, and who warrants intercession?

The Arabic word *shafa'a* means "a respected individual in the eyes of God," such as a prophet or infallible Imam, who can intercede for others to have their sins either forgiven or mitigated. Therefore, intercession is the act of a pious individual requesting forgiveness and mercy from God on behalf of someone who has sinned.

There is no doubt that God solely reserves the right to forgive us; and He is even closer to us than our jugular vein. However, God wants us to worship Him through the channel which He has prescribed for us. The Noble Qur'an shares with us an important story about Prophet Adam (a) and the angels, and this story sheds light on the concept of intercession.

---

[98] *Al-Amali*, by al-Sadouq, p. 159.

When God created Adam (a), He instructed the angels to prostrate to him. From the Qur'an:

So the angels fell prostrate (to Adam), all of them together. Save Iblis (Satan); he refused to be amongst those who prostrate.[118]

God chose Adam (a) to act as an intermediary between Him and the angels and demanded that they all turn to Adam (a) and prostrate themselves to him. Satan, whose arrogance surfaced, utterly refused, and he tried to negotiate another alternative with God. He asked God that if He spared him from prostrating to Adam (a), then he would worship God in a way that no other being has ever worshipped him like. God replied to him: "I wish to be worshipped the way I want."[119]

An important part of worshipping God is seeking the intercession of those whom He has appointed. By not seeking an intercessor, we will not have worshipped God the way He wants us to.

There are many important reasons why God has made intercession an integral part of faith, but we will only address two reasons here.

First, intercession is intended to show the status of an intercessor. Individuals such as Prophet Muhammad (ṣ) and Imam al-Husayn (a) achieved the epitome of sacrifice. The Prophet faced severe persecution from his relatives and countrymen. In Mecca, he was physically attacked, all sorts of heinous rumors and accusations were spread against him, he was financially boycotted,

---

[118] *Noble Qur'an*, Suratul Hijr (15), verses 30-31

[119] *Bihar al-anwar*, vol. 2, p. 262

socially isolated, and tens of battles were waged against him simply because he preached the message of God. Prophet Jesus (a) also faced extreme persecution because he preached God's message. Imam al-Husayn (a) offered everything he had in Karbala. He offered his life and blood, witnessed the massacre of his companions, suffered from unbearable thirst, witnessed his six-month-old baby slaughtered by a three-pronged arrow while in his arms, saw his eldest son and some seventeen members of his family killed in the battlefield, many of them dismembered, and he knew after his death his women and children would be attacked and beaten—all for the sake of God. Historians say that when he was breathing his final moments after he fell down from his horse, while sustaining hundreds of wounds, he said: "Oh God, I have accepted wholeheartedly what you have willed for me." Imam al-Husayn (a) also said these lines of poetry about the tragedy of Karbala:

Lord, I have deserted all of creation for Your love,

And I have orphaned my family so that I can meet You.

So if You dismember me into pieces in the way of Your love,

My heart will not sway an iota towards anyone else but You.

Imam al-Husayn (a) did not sacrifice all of this so that he would achieve a worldly position or assume temporal power. Charles Dickens has been reported to say: "If Husain fought to quench his worldly desires, (as alleged by certain Christian critics) then I do not understand why his sisters, wives and children accompanied him. It stands to reason therefore that he sacrificed purely for Islam."[120]

How can God reward Prophet Muhammad (ṣ) and Imam al-Husayn (a) for their sacrifices? Giving them the highest levels of paradise is not enough because they did not sacrifice in order to go to paradise - they did so purely for God.

The best and most just way God can reward them is by choosing them to be intermediaries and intercessors. In essence, God is telling us that if you want to come to Me, then you have to go through them, for they serve as God's gates. Is there an honor greater than being the gate of God? This is the only reward that can do justice to their mindboggling sacrifices. Thus, We can invoke God directly, but He has asked us to go through the gate which He has chosen.

The second reason is that God wants us to focus our attention on the intercessors and learn from them. When we are required to seek the prophets and Imams as intercessors, we are compelled to learn about them and implement their teachings in our lives. The closer we become to them, the more they will ask God to forgive us. This is indeed a fascinating way in which God guides us to obey His commands by referring us to those individuals who passed their test with utmost success in this transient life.

It is also important to note that while seeking the intercession of someone, we are not worshipping that person as we are only permitted to worship God. We are simply imploring the intercessor to ask God to help us and forgive us. Intercession is like

---

[120] http://en.wikipedia.org/wiki/Husayn_ibn_Ali#cite_note-43. Accessed 26 August 2012.

seeking a doctor when you become sick. We can directly ask God to heal us, but that may not always work because God himself has told us that when you get sick seek treatment and I will help you. The healer is neither the doctor nor the medication. God is the ultimate healer. You can say the pill has the power to heal, but only with the permission of God. Intercession is quite similar.

Let us take another example to be more familiar with the idea of intercession. Gaining the benefit of intercession is similar to having a cosigner for a bank loan. One person may have a strong credit, while another person does not. Because of the cosigner's stronger credit, the person with a weaker credit is able to get the loan. If we change *credit* to *piety* with God and change *loan* to *forgiveness,* then we describe the necessity of intercession with God. If I lack enough good deeds to achieve God's forgiveness, then the Prophet (ṣ) can intercede for me and make me eligible for God's forgiveness.

The intercessor must meet certain conditions, however. The conditions are that he or she must be a Muslim who believes in God and the prophets, and he or she must not have committed a major sin, such as ascribing a partner to God or committing an act of murder. Furthermore, any intercession must have God's approval and blessing. The Qur'an states:

Who is he that can intercede with Him but by His permission?[121]

Another Qur'anic verse says:

---

[121] *Noble Qur'an*, Suratul Baqarah (2), verse 255

On that day shall no intercession avail except of him whom the Beneficent God allows and whose word He is pleased with.[122]

Prophet Muhammad (ṣ) has the greatest ability to intercede and can do so for the largest number of people; but all of the other prophets and Imams also have the right to intercede.

Some narrations expand the power of intercession to any pious, God-fearing individual, perhaps for as many as three hundred or four hundred people. (Essentially, the higher an intercessor's position, the more people he can intercede for.)

However, we should remember that intercession is not intended to be a loophole for escaping our religious duties. Before his death, Imam Jafar al-Sadiq (a) said: "Our intercession will not include someone who disregards his prayers."

The Imam is teaching us that in order to be qualified for their intercession, we must make a sincere effort to do good deeds in this life and to also avoid committing sins. We must not neglect any religious duty and simply hope for intercession; and it is up to God to accept anyone's intercession. Muslims seeking forgiveness can only pray that God will permit the Prophet and his pure progeny to intercede for them on the Day of Judgment.

59. Do Muslims have a religious obligation to guide those who do not follow the right path?

Imam Ali (a) instructs us to educate the ignorant by saying: "You must guide the ignorant one who has gone astray."[123] It is the responsibility of all Muslims to educate their less-informed family

---

[122] *Noble Qur'an*, Surat Taha (20), verse 109

[123] *Awali al-Li'ali*, vol. 4, p. 79, Hadith no. 74

members, neighbors, and friends. God will definitely reward those Muslims who educate others.

One important narration relates to us that when Prophet Muhammad (ṣ) handed the banner of Islam to Imam Ali (a) and dispatched him to Yemen, the Prophet (ṣ) said to him:

> O Ali, do not fight them before you invite them to Islam. I swear by the One who sent me as a Prophet, that if God guides one individual through you it is better for you than if you own everything that the sun shines upon.[124]

There is another narration that says religion simply means offering advice to others for the sake of God, the Almighty.[125]

It is crucial that one offers his sincere advice to a misled Muslim brother or sister, and to all of humanity. We must help others correct their mistakes, change their paths, and encourage them to follow the right direction.

Prophet Muhammad (ṣ) has been reported as saying: "A believer is the mirror of another believer."[126] A mirror simply reflects our physical features whether they are pleasant or unpleasant. Similarly, a Muslim must act as a mirror for other Muslims—politely and appropriately pointing out their faults and ultimately offering to help rectify and guide them.

If you realize that someone is in danger, would you not feel obligated to advise that person and inform him that he is in danger? If one is lost, is it not our obligation to guide that person if

---

[124] *Al-Kafi*, vol. 5, p. 28

[125] *Bihar al-Anwar*, vol. 64, p. 273

[126] *Kanz al-Ummal*, vol. 1, p. 141

we can? There is nothing more important than our fate in the Hereafter because it will determine whether we will be in perpetual bliss or in eternal misery. Therefore, if you see someone going astray, then try to help him by saving him from eternal misery.

60. Should a Muslim report another Muslim to the authorities for breaking the law of the land?

According to the mainstream scholars of Islam, breaking any law is not permissible. All Muslims are required to abide by the laws of the land in which they reside. If breaking the law involves endangering the lives of innocent people or harming the property of innocent people, then one should inform the authorities.

61. I have been told that hurting oneself is prohibited (haram). Wouldn't this suggest that the rituals in commemoration of Imam al-Husayn (a), which sometimes involve hitting one's head with a blade, are prohibited?

God says in the Qur'an:

> And spend in the way of God and cast not yourselves to perdition with your own hands, and do good (to others); surely God loves the doers of good."[127]

This verse means that one should not cause one's own destruction or cause extreme harm to oneself.

Muslim scholars believe that intentional, extreme, or self-inflicted harm is prohibited, especially if it leads to one's demise. It is on this basis that Muslim scholars believe using drugs is

---

[127] Noble Qur'an, Suratul Baqarah (2), verse 195

prohibited. However, there has been debate about how extreme the harm must be in order for it to be considered as impermissible. For example, eating a meal saturated with oil can increase cholesterol, but this might not be deemed harmful enough for scholars to prohibit it.

The act of hitting of oneself with a blade (referred to in the Arabic culture as *tatbeer*) is a tradition practiced during the commemoration of Ashura by some members who follow the school of Ahlul Bayt. It has been a controversial subject among the scholars themselves, and some scholars believe that hitting oneself with a blade is not prohibited unless is leads to permanent damage or death (which is rarely the case).

Therefore, minor bloodletting during the commemorations of Ashura may not constitute enough harm to warrant prohibition. Scholars who accept this view cite many other Islamic rituals which involve extreme hardship but are not deemed as sins, such as fasting during long summer days during the month of Ramadhan, or going to *hajj* when it required a prolonged, difficult, and perilous journey. These scholars deem *tatbeer* a way to sympathize with the holy family of the Prophet during the mourning period of the tragic events of Karbala.

Other scholars believe that this act is prohibited not only based on extreme harm to the body but also its potential to generate negative views about Islam, Shi'ism, and Imam al-Husayn's (a) revolution. They believe that, given hostile attitudes toward Islam during the last few decades and its depiction in the Western media as pro-violence, the Ashura rituals may invite further criticism of Islam.

62. Why does Islam condone capital punishment?

Islam has permitted capital punishment for murderers because Islam is a pro-life religion. Islam believes deeply in the sanctity of life. The Qur'an considers killing one innocent person to be equivalent to killing all of humanity:

> For this reason did We prescribe to the children of Israel that whoever slays a soul, unless it be for manslaughter or for mischief in the land, it is as though he has killed all of humanity; and whoever keeps it (as much as one person) alive, it is as though he kept alive all of humanity.[128]

Therefore, enforcing capital punishment by killing a murderer is the best deterrent for other murders to take place. It discourages would-be murders from taking innocent lives. Nothing else can stop a murderer from killing innocent people as much as knowing that his own life will be taken once he engages in killing innocent people. God says in the Qur'an:

> And there is life for you in (the law of) retaliation, O people of understanding, that you may guard yourselves.[129]

Islam does believe in mercy and forgiveness, but Islam also knows that nothing can encourage a murderer to commit further murders more than leniency. There is a Persian expression that says, "Showing mercy and compassion to a wolf is indeed an injustice to the sheep."

---

[128] *Noble Qur'an*, Suratul Ma'idah (5), verse 32
[129] *Noble Qur'an*, Suratul Baqarah (2), verse 179

People with criminal records, especially those who have committed murders, will likely take pardoning them as a green light to commit further crimes. The best way to stop these murderers is by putting an end to their lives, so that other innocent people are not killed.

Some people may argue that executing a murderer will not bring the victim back to life and therefore capital punishment should be banned. The idea of capital punishment is not to bring a victim back, for obviously that is not possible, but it is to deter other potential murderers from preying upon more innocent victims.

While the deterrence effect of capital punishment is debated in our society, Islam believes that if a society's justice system is fair and effective, then the death penalty will undoubtedly have a strong deterrence effect.

There are many glitches in our modern justice system. Not all victims are treated equally, as certain groups and minorities are treated differently. Institutional racism is widespread in our society. Those who have money to hire influential lawyers can sometimes find their way out even if they are guilty. Sitting on death row for long years (sometimes decades) also diminishes the deterrence effect. Islam believes that once there is indisputable evidence that someone has committed murder, then the death penalty should be executed without much delay. Murderers who know that if they get caught they will immediately be executed are deterred much more than murderers who know that if they get caught they will spend an unknown number of years in prison before being possibly executed.

Statistics on the rate of crime reveal that there are problems with our justice system and society. According to the U.S. Department of Justice, Bureau of Justice Statistics, at the end of 2006, there were over 2.25 million prisoners held in federal, state, or local prisons. In addition, there was an annual growth rate in the number of prisoners of 3.4 percent since 1995. The United States is the wealthiest, most technologically advanced, and most economically innovative country in the world, yet these figures demonstrate we have a problem and that the current justice system must be improved.

While Islam condones capital punishment for murderers, Islam is more concerned about addressing and correcting the root causes of crime in society. Poverty, discrimination, racism, and other factors all contribute to crime. Addressing these problems is a greater Islamic priority than implementing the death penalty.

It is worth noting that many people assume capital punishment to be very cruel and that a life sentence in prison is better. This is not necessarily the case, however. Locking up someone for fifty years may in fact be worse, because freedom is amongst the most valuable privileges or rights that we have. Patrick Henry famously said, "Give me liberty or give me death." Being imprisoned for a lifetime goes against the very essence of our humanity. And it does not help criminals. Rather, it makes inmates more psychologically ill. Many inmates end up committing further crimes once they are released. Death however, is a transition from this life to the next; and once criminals are put to death, then God will judge them, and He is the most Just.

Despite allowing capital punishment, Islam still gives the guardian of a victim the right to pardon the murderer. Many murderers have been pardoned by the loved ones of their victims. However, Islam believes that the judge still has the right to prosecute the murderer even after being pardoned by the guardian of a victim. Scholars cite what is known in Islamic jurisprudence as the private right and the public right. The guardian can relinquish his own private right to eliminate the life of a murderer, but as the guardian of a society, a judge still maintains the public right to take the life of a murderer, if he deems fit.

63. How does Islam view suicide?

Suicide is an extremely grave sin in the eyes of God. Indeed it is not so different from homicide. God says in the Qur'an:

> And they who do not call upon another god with God and do not slay the soul, which God has forbidden except in the requirements of justice, and (who) do not commit fornication and he who does this shall find a requital of sin. The punishment shall be doubled to him on the day of resurrection, and he shall abide therein in abasement.[130]

> O you who believe! Do not devour your property among yourselves falsely, except that it be trading by your mutual consent; and do not kill yourselves; surely Allah is Merciful to you.[131]

---

[130] *Noble Qur'an*, Suratul Furqan (25), verses 68–69

[131] *Noble Qur'an*, Suratul Nisa (4), verse 29

God has permitted human beings control over their bodies, limbs, and organs in a way that benefits them and ensures their survival, but humans are not permitted to terminate their own lives.

Those who commit suicide, however, are still eligible for God's mercy (especially if they were under extreme circumstances that effectively altered their state of mind to the extent that they did not really realize what they were doing). God's mercy may not mean that they will escape punishment, but they may receive a lesser punishment. However, if they lost complete sense before committing suicide, then many scholars believe that they will be retested by God on the Day of Judgment, or they may be forgiven. Also, committing suicide does not negate an individual's Muslim status—one will still be treated as a Muslim afterwards.

64. What is the Islamic perspective on *khums* and *zakat*, and what is the difference between the two?

Charity (*khums*) and alms (*zakat*) are both mandatory Islamic financial obligations.

Zakat is paid on nine items: sheep, camels, cows, wheat, barley, raisins, rice, gold and silver. Muslims must pay on these items only if they own certain amounts of them. For example, if someone owns at least forty sheep, then he must pay the equivalent of one sheep as *zakat*.

In the Qur'an, God explains how *zakat* is to be dispersed:

Alms are only for the poor and the needy, and the officials (appointed) over them, and those whose hearts are made to incline (to truth) and the (ransoming of) captives and those in debts and in the way of Allah and the wayfarer; an ordinance from Allah; and Allah is knowing, Wise.[132]

With the exception of gold and silver, the items subject to mandatory *zakat* relate to agriculture. Those who do not live in agricultural societies must only pay *khums*, which literally means "one-fifth." God states in the Qur'an:

And know that whatever thing you gain, a fifth of it is for God and for the Messenger and for the near of kin and the orphans and the needy and the wayfarer.[133]

Khums is a mandatory tax that each Muslim individual must pay on his or her net savings. It is 20 percent of one's net income. For example, if an individual makes $60,000 a year and his yearly expenditures are $50,000 (and thus he saves $10,000), this person must pay $2,000 *khums*, or 20% of the $10,000 net savings.

According to scholars, *khums* must also be paid on our excess or unused items. For example, if a person buys or is gifted a shirt but does not wear it for over a year, then he is liable for *khums* (20%) on the value of the shirt. The same ruling can be applied to excess food or other goods which a person accumulates throughout the year in excess of his needs. However, for the specifics on how these are calculated, one should refer to his or her religious authority.

Muslim scholars indicate that *khums* should be dispersed in the following manner:

---

[132] *Noble Qur'an*, Suratul Tawbah (9), verse 60
[133] *Noble Qur'an*, Suratul Anfal (8), verse 41

- Half of the *khums* that a person pays is called the Imam's share. It is given to the infallible Imam so he can disperse it to various charitable projects and the Muslim welfare system. In the absence of an infallible Imam (such as in our times, as Imam al-Mahdi (a) is in occultation), this portion is handed to his representative, who is the highest Muslim scholar, known as a *Marja'*. The *Marja'* spends the Imam's share on charitable foundations and projects, such as students of the Islamic seminaries, charitable hospitals, orphanages, Islamic libraries, Islamic propagation, and needy Muslims.

- The second half is given to needy descendants of Hashim, the family of the Prophet, because the Hashimites are prohibited from receiving mandatory *zakat*. Also, as the descendants and relatives of the Prophet, God decided to honor their dignity by not allowing them to become beggars in a Muslim society.

Muslims may directly give part of the Imam's share to charitable causes such as building mosques, orphanages, clinics, and Islamic schools only with the permission of their respective scholars.

Some scholars who do not follow the school of *Ahlul Bayt* believe that *khums* applies only to war spoils. Yet in the above-mentioned verse in the Qur'an, God clearly indicates that *khums* is not only restricted to war spoils. Everything that we gain is subject to *khums*, including our income.

65. What does Islam say about buying lottery tickets which are prevalent in the West?

A lottery is deemed by many Muslim scholars to be a form of gambling, and Islam is known to prohibit gambling. However, if an individual buys a lottery ticket intending to help a charitable cause (a school or hospital fund-raiser, for example) rather than to win a prize, then this is a form of donation, not gambling. Buying a lottery ticket to win a prize is a form of gambling and is entirely prohibited.

Note that *accepting* a prize, should one win, is not an issue. Muslims can lawfully accept a prize regardless of their motivation. As far as winning the prize, both groups—those who bought the lottery with the intention of gambling and those who bought the ticket with the intention of donating to a charitable cause—can accept the prize lawfully should they win. The reason for this is because the law of the land considers giving this prize legitimate, and therefore accepting the prize is not problematic, just like receiving interest from non-Muslim banks is legitimate as the law of the land allows it.

In conclusion, buying lottery tickets itself is prohibited if it is done with the intention of winning the lottery. If not, then it is not prohibited. In both cases, obtaining the prize is not prohibited, and taking the prize is legitimate.

It is worth mentioning that some people buy lottery tickets with the intention of winning the prize and using it for charitable causes such as building mosques or Islamic schools. These good intentions, however, do not legitimize the buying of a lottery ticket. Since the intent of purchasing a ticket is to win a prize, then it is considered gambling in Islam.

66. What does Islam say about dealing with interest?

All Muslims scholars believe that even though interest (riba) is strictly prohibited in Islam, there are certain exceptions in which it is allowed.

One exception is when dealing with non-Muslims. A Muslim can receive interest from a non-Muslim bank; and the rationale behind this is a narration that specifically indicates the permissibility of a Muslim receiving interest from a non-Muslim. The narration says, "There shall be no harm from a Muslim receiving interest from a non-Muslim." [134] In addition, there is a basic Islamic law saying that you can hold non-Muslims to their own laws, and since non-Muslims in general do not see harm in dealing with usury, thus Muslims are permitted to receive this kind of interest.

If Muslims own a bank, it is still permissible for Muslim customers to collect interest on their savings accounts as long as they do not stipulate that earning interest is their reason for opening the savings account. (Some of our scholars, however, dispute this and state that since this essentially amounts to collecting interest then it is not permissible). Simply put, in Islam, earning interest becomes prohibited when it is the motivation for conducting a business transaction.

It has been narrated that in numerous cases, Prophet Muhammad (ṣ) repaid a lender more than what he owed him. It is

---

[134] *Wasa'el al-Shia*, vol. 12 p. 437, chapter 5, hadith 7

in fact recommended (*mustahab*) to pay back more than the original loan that a person gave you as a gesture of appreciation to the lender who offered you a non-interest loan. However, one must simply avoid stipulating the earning of interest when giving a loan.

67. Many Muslims buy homes through a mortgage system and borrow money from the bank. Given that interest is forbidden in Islam, is this permissible?

Muslim scholars offer two ways for Muslims living in the West to buy a house using the mortgage system lawfully and permissibly.

The first is through what scholars call *istinqath*. This means that when Muslims apply for a loan from a non-Muslim bank, they simply consider the loan that they are taking as money which they own. However, the payments, which include the interest, must still be paid on that loan simply because Muslims must abide by the law of the land. It is not permissible to go against the law of the land. This is like tax money which a Muslim in the West must pay to the government; for there is no other legal choice but to pay the taxes.

The second scenario is called a credit (*salaf*) sale. This means that the Muslim buyer of a new house would include the entire amount of interest to be paid over the life of the loan in the price of the house. For example, if the price of a house is $100,000 and the interest that one will have to pay over fifteen years will be $50,000, then the buyer would consider the price of the house to be $150,000, rather than $100,000. The Muslim buyer in this way will not be paying interest at all. Rather, he or she will be purchasing the house for a price higher than the one written on the purchase agreement. The perceived interest plus the original price of the house becomes the new price of the house.

This, of course, negates the use of adjustable-rate mortgages, as it is necessary to know the full amount of the interest to be paid over the life of the loan in order to calculate the true price of the house. The total price of the house must be known at the time of purchasing the house in order for the transaction to be rendered Islamically valid. This transaction is very similar to buying a car. Car buyers usually have two basic options: buy the car in cash for around $10,000, or pay in monthly installments that will total about $13,000. In the second case, the buyer is not paying interest, but has to pay a higher price because he could not pay the full amount in cash.

68. Are Muslims allowed to participate in political elections or run for political office in the West?

There are more than 20 million Muslims who now live in the West, in Europe and North America. These Muslims cannot afford to be passive or indifferent towards their respective countries' affairs. Those who do not participate in the political process, including elections, exclude themselves from the larger society and unnecessarily deny themselves many rights. Muslims in the West pay taxes and therefore have a say in how their tax money should be dispersed. This cannot be achieved without political participation.

However, Muslim scholars set forth two conditions for Muslims participating in elections and seeking political office:

> 1. Muslims, once running for office or participating in elections, must seek Islamic interests, such as the higher

interest of the Muslim community, and not their own personal interests. Islamic interests include working for justice, providing a solution for poverty, crime and corruption, protecting the rights of Muslims, countering Islamophobia, and putting an end to global wars and violence.

2. Muslim scholars living in the West with political expertise must verify these interests.

If these two conditions are met, then Muslims not only are allowed to participate in elections and seek official positions, but are even recommended to do so.

We must understand that in order for Muslims in the West to gain power, prominence, and influence in their respective societies, they need to be competitive and politically savvy. They need to engage in the same process that has enabled other minorities to pursue their political, social, and economic aspirations.

69. Is it permissible to sell pork, alcohol, or non-*halal* meats in a non-Muslim country?

All Muslim scholars uphold the decision that selling alcohol is forbidden in all cases and under all circumstances, regardless of the nation's predominant faith. The same holds true for selling pork; it is totally forbidden. As for non-*halal* meats (meats not slaughtered in the prescribed Islamic manner), it is permissible to sell them only to non-Muslims.

70. Although men are not allowed to wear silk, can they sleep or pray on silk?

A man is prohibited from wearing pure silk. Wearing pure silk during the prayer will even invalidate that prayer. However, praying on a silk rug or sleeping on silk bed sheets is not prohibited (*haram*). What is prohibited is simply wearing it. Other uses of silk are not prohibited.

For clothing, only pure silk is prohibited; therefore, clothes that are made of a combination of silk and other fabrics are not prohibited. This stipulation applies only to men as women are permitted to wear pure silk, both during prayer and elsewhere.

In addition to silk, yellow gold of any karat is also not permissible for men to wear during prayers or at any other time. Wearing yellow gold during the prayer will invalidate it as well. The only exception is having teeth made of gold.

White gold, however, is not prohibited, and the wearing of any other jewelry, such as diamonds, rubies, or silver, is also not prohibited for men.

71. Is getting a tattoo allowed? If so, can Muslims get a tattoo of the Qur'an or God's name?

Tattoos in general are not prohibited in Islam even though Muslims must treat their bodies as a trust and a gift from God. We are supposed to do our best to maintain them in the right and proper manner. They are instruments of our survival, and we are obligated to take care of them in a way that ensures our safety, health, and well-being. Tattoos become problematic in three scenarios:

Temporary tattoos could prevent water from reaching the skin during ablution (*wudhu*) and ceremonial showers (*ghusl*).

Permanent tattoos, whose inks are underneath the skin, don't interfere this way, but could present another problem with their permanence. Getting a tattoo with the word *God* or any of His sacred names, the name of a prophet, or the name of an infallible Imam is *haram* because we are not perpetually in a clean state (this is for the name of God in any language and the same holds true for the names of the prophets or Imams in any language). Someone with such a tattoo cannot always be in a state of ritual purity and thus is committing a sin.

A third problem with tattoos arises if a female has to expose her body to a male tattoo artist who is not allowed to see her uncovered body, or the reverse scenario, when a female must touch a male's body to create the tattoo. Both are absolutely prohibited (*haram*) in Islam. However, if the tattoo artist is of the same gender and the private parts do not get exposed at all during the process of getting a tattoo, then this problem is resolved.

72. Are Muslims forbidden to touch dogs?

The issues surrounding dogs in Islam are strictly hygienic. Touching a dog is not forbidden at all when both the animal and one's hands are dry - there is no need to even wash one's hands or clothes in this case. But if the dog or a person's hands are wet, then whatever area comes into contact with the dog must be washed with water.

Keeping a dog in a Muslim household is not prohibited, however it is something which is not recommended. It has been narrated that the angels do not enter into a house in which there is a dog.[135]

This is not to call dogs evil, for dogs are not evil creatures. They are a creation of God, and they exhibit noble characteristics. However, they may carry germs and viruses from which Islam intends to protect people. God knows best.

73. If God proclaimed that His word cannot be changed, then why did He "permit" changes in the Torah and Bible?

God did not say that His *word* couldn't be changed—He said that the *Qur'an* cannot be changed. A passage in the Qur'an states:

> Surely We have revealed the Reminder (The Qur'an), and We will most surely be its guardian.[136]

Nowhere in the Qur'an does it say that the other holy books cannot be altered.

So why did God preserve the original content of the Qur'an and not the Torah or the Bible?

God tested ancient nations on their attitudes toward the divine texts and found that some of them did not duly guard their sacred meanings. Some Jews and Christians throughout history tampered with their divine books.

The Qur'an, which is the final revelation and summary of all of the Divine messages, includes the essential teachings of the previous books, and so God saw fit to protect it, and by extension, the original Torah and Bible.

---

[135] *Al-Kafi*, vol. 3, p. 393

[136] *Noble Qur'an*, Suratul Hijr (15), verse 9

74. What is the significance of the daily prayers (Salat)?

Prayer (*salat*) has been described by Prophet Muhammad (ṣ) in one narration as the ascension of a believer.[148] This narration may sum up its significance as it shows the symbolic gesture that Muslims perform to connect us with our Lord.

Prayer has been depicted by the Qur'an, the Prophet, and Imams as the "connecting channel" between God and us. Also, the Qur'an speaks about the significant moral role prayer plays in our lives. For example, God says in the Qur'an that prayer forbids indecency and evil:

> *Recite that which has been revealed to you of the Book and keep up prayer; surely prayer keeps (one) away from indecency and evil, and certainly the remembrance of God is the greatest, and God knows what you do.*[149]

In other words, once a person fully engages in prayer and focuses on the purposes of prayer, then his or her prayer will be the best deterrent for committing any sins.

When a person addresses God numerous times every day in his prayer by saying, "Only You do we worship and only You do we seek help from," then this person is declaring his or her deep commitment to the obedience of God only. Therefore, scholars believe that this prayer, by its very nature, cleanses the soul of the believer.

Another benefit prayer may offer is washing off the sins of the person who offers the prayers on a regular basis. In this regards,

---

[148] *Mustadrak Safinat al-Bihar*, vol. 6, p. 343

[149] *Noble Qur'an*, Suratul Ankbaut (29), verse 45

the Prophet offered the following analogy in which he said to a group of his companions: "If one of your neighbors had a river flowing next to his house and he rinsed himself five times a day in that river, then do you think that there would be any filth left on his body?" They all replied no. The Prophet continued and said that the same holds true for the prayer. When a person prays five times a day sincerely to God, then his prayers will entitle him to God's forgiveness. Therefore, his sins will be washed off."[150]

This is also supported by a verse in the Qur'an that says the prayer on the two sides of the day—meaning in the morning (fajr) and at sunset (maghrib)—will definitely take the sins away, by the virtue of the blessings of these prayers.

> And keep up prayer in the two parts of the day and in the first hours of the night; surely good deeds take away evil deeds this is a reminder to the mindful.[151]

Prayer, therefore, is the most profound devotional act that a Muslim can perform. According to one narration, it is the distinctive thin line that separates a believer from belief and disbelief.[152] It is the safety valve that deters a Muslim from falling into the pit of despair or deviating from the path of God. It is also the pillar of faith by which a Muslim individual is identified.

Finally, it is the last thing which all of the prophets and Imams advised their followers to perform when they offered their last will and testament, either written or verbal.

---

[150] *Bihar al-anwar*, vol. 79, p. 236

[151] *Noble Qur'an*, Surat Hud (11), verse 114

[152] *Mizan al-Hikmah*, vol. 3, p. 1644

Medical Ethics

75. When does a fetus acquire a soul?

Islamically, it has been mentioned that at four months, the child acquires life. Whether this is a literal or symbolic length of time is debatable. Some believe this is literal, and some believe it is symbolic and that life begins at conception. Four months is when a fetus starts moving in the womb; it could also be a reference to a child's full development, as it is believed that the body becomes fully formed during the fourth month.

76. Is abortion allowed in Islam?

The majority of Muslim scholars believe that aborting a fetus at any time is prohibited, except when the life of the mother is in jeopardy.

A few scholars believe that aborting the fetus before four months is permissible if the mother is experiencing physical or moral hardship, as in the case of conception due to having been raped. This may bring unbearable long-term emotional suffering and stigma.

However, the majority of scholars stress that aborting a fetus is absolutely prohibited, unless keeping the fetus poses a grave danger to the life of the mother.

77. If abortion has already occurred, then what are the repercussions?

Muslim scholars distinguish between aborting directly and aborting indirectly.

Direct abortion means that the mother takes pills or commits an act to intentionally miscarry a fetus. In this case, the mother must pay retribution (*diyyah*). This retribution money is similar to "blood money" that is paid directly to the heirs of the fetus.

The value of the retribution depends on the fetus's age at the time of abortion.

If the fetus was four weeks or younger, then the retribution (*diyyah*) is twenty gold dinars, which is equivalent to eighty grams of gold. If the price of gold is approximately $20 per gram, then the retribution for abortion from zero to four weeks would be $1,600.

If the fetus is four to eight weeks, then it is forty dinars, equivalent to 160 grams of gold, or about $3,200.

From eight to twelve weeks, it is sixty dinars, which is 240 grams of gold, or approximately $4,800.

From twelve to sixteen weeks, it is eighty dinars, or 320 grams gold, which is about $6,400.

At sixteen weeks, it is 100 dinars, or about 360 grams of gold, which is about $7,200.

Thereafter, it is one thousand dinars, which is four thousand grams of gold, or about $80,000.

Indirect abortion is if a physician aborts the fetus, in which case there is no longer retribution required to be paid by the mother; rather, it is on the executer of the abortion. However, even though the mother is not obligated to pay the retribution, she is still viewed as an accomplice to murder. Unless she seeks sincere forgiveness, she will be viewed as a sinner in the eyes of God.

78. What does Islam say about organ donation and acceptance?

The rules that regulate organ donations are divided into two scenarios. The first occurs in life, and the second occurs after death.

During a person's lifetime, a Muslim can donate an organ only if that organ is not external, such as an eye, ear, nose, or hand. In addition, the donor's life cannot depend on it (such as a liver or a heart). Therefore, internal and non-essential organs are permissible to donate. One example of this is a single kidney. Because it is an internal organ and one's life is not dependent upon it, then it may be donated.

After death, a Muslim can donate any part of his body, external or internal, as long as it was stipulated in his or her own will. A parent, son, or wife cannot make the decision to donate the deceased's organ without the deceased permitting it in a will.

Some scholars believe that in all three cases or scenarios the recipient must be Muslim.

79. What does Islam say about withholding or withdrawing life support?

Mainstream Muslim scholars believe that using and maintaining life support for a patient who is in need is mandatory. It would be a sin not to put the patient on life support or a resuscitating machine if the patient needs it to remain alive. Some scholars even believe that doctors and physicians who remove patients from life support, with the result being death, are murderers in the eyes of God. A few scholars believe that it is not mandatory to put a patient on life support, but once someone is on life support, then there can be no denying him the right to continue being on it, regardless of the prognosis.

The quality of life is not an issue. From an Islamic perspective, human life is sacred regardless of the level—a vegetative state or in full dynamic terms. All necessary techniques such as CPR, mechanical ventilation, and electrical shock are mandatory once deemed vital to the survival of a patient.

The only debate that may come up is whether it is necessary for the relatives of a patient diagnosed as brain dead to continue life support or not. Again, the majority of Muslim scholars believe that it is mandatory and that the relatives of a patient should do everything possible to prevent any attempt to remove the patient from life support until complete death comes (when a patient's heart stops and some or all of the death signs appear).

An important point to consider is that although a person is pronounced brain dead by doctors, the soul might still be attached to the body. The soul has its own dimensions, and we do not have a full grasp of it. Therefore, removing a person from life support may involve harmful effects upon the soul.

Some narrations indicate that the soul of a dying person is being purified, so it must be left up to God to "pull the final plug." Furthermore, sometimes doctors pronounce a person brain dead but they really are not and they can be in a deep coma. There have been cases of people regaining consciousness after being considered brain dead. Keeping life support on will ensure that the person was given a full chance to survive.

Some argue that keeping patients on life support exhausts and drains our resources. If in a given society keeping a patient on life support will indeed exhaust the resources to the extent that other living people will be deprived from being treated and saved, then scholars may allow the removal of it in order to save the lives of other human beings.

For instance, assume that a hospital can only admit one patient to its intensive care unit, but we have two patients who require such care. The first is a brain dead patient who requires life support, and the other is a patient who had an accident and needs an operation to survive. Given that the chances of saving the second person are much higher than the patient who is pronounced brain dead, then it becomes mandatory to save the life of the second person.

A minority of scholars, however, believe that a brain dead patient is dead. In their view, the signs of life are not real. It is the life of cells and not the person himself. This group of scholars believes that it is not necessary to go through the inconvenience of putting a patient who is clinically dead on life support.

A living will made by a Muslim in the West must not include any article or clause that conflicts with the tenets of Islam. Islamically speaking, the relatives of an incapacitated patient should not implement parts of a living will if they conflict with the teachings and edicts of the scholars of Islam. They should follow the rulings of their respective scholar. It is mandatory for the relatives to respect, honor, and implement wills as long as they do not conflict with the teachings of Islam.

80. What is the Islamic perspective on cloning?

Muslim scholars believe that partial cloning of human organs, such as a heart, kidney, or liver for the purpose of transplantation for treatment is permissible. A big debate is sparked, however, as soon as one talks about cloning a fully formed human being. Many scholars believe this is problematic for certain reasons:

1. If cloning was permitted, then it might open the door for a tyrant or ill-wisher who wants to clone people for devious purposes. It has been historically reported that the dictator Hitler was seeking methods with which he could clone himself. This could endanger millions of innocent people and the very future of humanity.

2. Scholars point out that a person who has been cloned may not recognize a father or mother, and for that matter, any family members. This is a deviation from the normal structure God has drawn for human reproduction. This person may therefore lack the affection that is needed to grow up healthy and functional in a stable family.

3. Cloning a fully formed human being would require methods that are totally abnormal. It is does not involve a male and a female in a natural process of reproduction. It involves a cell that is taken from any part of a male or female and is instilled in the woman's egg. Theoretically, a woman could be a father and a mother at the same time. For these reasons and many

others, the majority of Muslims scholars have skeptical views about cloning full human beings.

Some Shia Muslim scholars believe that if cloning does not present any dangers and is not used for ill purposes, then it would be permitted.

Interfaith Questions

81. Do Jews, Christians, and Muslims all believe in the same God?

It seems that Muslims, Christians, and Jews all believe in the same God. They only differ in the naming of God—He could be called God, Allah, or Yahweh. Whatever name the People of the Book give Him, they seem to be speaking about the same God. The difference is in ascribing a partner to Him. Muslims believe that God has no partner whatsoever. He does not beget, nor is He begotten. The unity of God is the cornerstone of Islamic doctrine. Contemporary Jews also are known to believe in one God without believing in a partner to Him. However, according to the Qur'an, Jews believed that God has a son. God says in the Qur'an:

> *And the Jews say: Ezra is the son of God; and the Christians say: the Messiah is the son of God; these are the words of their mouths; they imitate the saying of those who disbelieved before; may God fight them; how they are turned away![207]*

It seems that at the time the Qur'an was revealed, mainstream Jews believed that Ezra was the son of God. Ezra was a Judaic figure who was known as the preserver of the Torah when the temple

---

[207] *Noble Qur'an*, Suratul Tawbah (9), verse 30

was destroyed during the invasion of Nebuchadnezzar II in 586 BC.[208]

Islam firmly asserts that God is **not** a physical entity; and therefore, Islam rejects attributing anthropomorphic qualities to God. If God were a physical being or possessed corporeal qualities, then He would be limited and in need of something. All physical beings, for instance, need space. God is above the physical world, and He is not in need of anything.

82. Will Jews and Christians also go to heaven?

A verse in the Qur'an says:

> Surely those who believe, and those who are Jews, and the Christians, and the Sabians, whoever believes in God and the Last Day and does good, they shall have their reward from their Lord, and there is no fear for them, nor shall they grieve.[209]

Most Muslim commentators believe that this verse refers to Jews who followed Judaism before the advent of Prophet Jesus (a), and Christians who followed Prophet Jesus (a) before Islam came. The Qur'an also says:

> And whoever desires a religion other than Islam, it shall not be accepted from him, and in the hereafter he will be one of the losers.[210]

---

[208] *Noble Qur'an*, commentary of Suratul Isra (17), verse 4, note no. 2174 (A. Yusuf Ali).

[209] *Noble Qur'an*, Suratul Baqarah (2), verse 62

[210] *Noble Qur'an*, Surat Aale Imran (3), verse 85

One grave sin that God will not forgive on the Day of Judgment, according to the Qur'an, is ascribing a partner to God:

> Surely God does not forgive that anything should be associated with Him, and forgives what is besides that to whomsoever He pleases; and whoever associates anything with God, he devises indeed a great sin.[211]

This verse implies that those who ascribe a partner to God and insist on doing so, even after knowing that it is a grave sin, may not be eligible for God's forgiveness. However, Muslims also believe in God's mercy and affection. God may exercise His power and discretion to forgive or not forgive whomever He wills.

Furthermore, Muslim philosophers believe that breaking one's promise is extremely inappropriate if the promise involves a reward. However, if the promise involves a punishment, it is not inappropriate to break that promise. For example, if a father promises his son that if he behaves he will buy him candy, then not buying him candy if he behaves is an injustice in the eyes of society. But if the father warns his son that if he misbehaves he will punish him, but then decides to forgive him even though he misbehaves and does not punish him, then this it is not deemed injustice. Therefore, Muslims believe that even though God has promised to not forgive those who ascribe a partner to Him, it does not negate the possibility that God may forgive them, if He feels fit to do so.

---

[211] *Noble Qur'an*, Suratul Nisa (4), verse 48

It is also worth mentioning that Muslim scholars divide polytheists (those who ascribe partners to God) into two categories: ignorant at fault and ignorant not at fault.

Ignorant at fault are those who have access to knowledge and the truth. An American citizen cannot use ignorance of tax laws as an excuse for not paying his or her due taxes. Similarly, a professor who teaches at an American university and has access to the truth about God and the divine faith of Islam cannot cite his ignorance of it as an excuse.

People who are ignorant but not at fault are those who have never had the chance to learn anything about God, Islam, or the ultimate truth. Those born and raised in a society that lacked opportunities for learning and studying other religions, including Islam, may fall into this category.

Muslim scholars draw a conclusion that God will not treat these two groups equally. He may well hold the first type responsible for their willful ignorance, while He might be more lenient with the second group.

We have narrations from the Ahlul Bayt that state on the Day of Judgment, God will retest those who were not at fault. If they pass that test, then they will be saved. We human beings lack the full capacity to determine who is at fault and who is not. Only God can make this judgment, and His judgment is undoubtedly based on complete justice and fairness for everyone.

83. Does Islam recognize the Christian and Hebrew scriptures as inspired texts? If so, should Muslims read, study, and pray over these texts?

Islam believes in the originality of the Torah and Bible. In other words, Muslims believe that God revealed the original texts of these scriptures.

The Torah was revealed to Prophet Moses (a). God says in the Qur'an:

Surely We revealed the Torah in which was guidance and light.[212]

The Bible was revealed to Prophet Jesus (a). God says in the Qur'an:

And We sent after them in their footsteps Jesus, son of Mary, verifying what was before him of the Torah and We gave him the Evangel in which was guidance and light, and verifying what was before it of Torah and a guidance and an admonition for those who guard (against evil).[213]

God also says in the Qur'an:

He has revealed to you the Book with truth, verifying that which is before it, and He revealed the Torah and the Evangel aforetime, a guidance for the people, and He sent the Furqan.[214]

However, Muslims believe that the Torah and Bible unfortunately have been tampered with since their revelation and are ultimately distorted. Not only Muslims, but even Biblical scholars have pointed out that extensive editing has been made to the Bible

---

[212] *Noble Qur'an*, Suratul Ma'idah (5), verse 44

[213] *Noble Qur'an*, Suratul Ma'idah (5), verse 46

[214] *Noble Qur'an*, Suratul Aale Imran (3), verse 3

since its revelation. Many chapters of the Bible are not the direct word of Prophet Jesus (a) and were compiled many years after him.

Substantial portions of the Torah and the Bible are still authentic and contain God's words, and Muslims regard parts of them as inspiring. However, Muslims believe that when the Qur'an was revealed, it replaced the two previous books.

With all due respect to the Bible and Torah, the Qur'an became the final divine word as to the direction set by God for humanity. To state it succinctly, the validity of the two earlier texts, despite their sanctity and originality, has expired, and they no longer need be followed after the revelation of the Qur'an.

For Muslims, there is no harm in reading or studying the Torah and Bible as long as they are aware of the context of the books' revelation and validity. Reading and studying the two texts accurately and critically will in fact prove that both of them had foretold the coming of Prophet Muhammad (ṣ). The Qur'an states:

> Those who follow the Messenger, the 'unlettered', whom they find written down with them in the Torah and the Evangel...[215]

The Torah and Bible include many verses, maxims and wisdom that any self-conscious human being would find inspiring.

As for praying, Muslims are obligated to pray exactly the way they have been instructed by the Qur'an and the narrations of Prophet Muhammad (ṣ) and his pure progeny. Therefore, no other text can substitute for the Qur'an as a book of guidance.

---

[215] *Noble Qur'an*, Suratul A'raf (7), verse 157

Family & Gender Issues

84. Can Muslim women take an active role in government, politics, and student leadership?

Muslim women may take an active role in government, politics, and student leadership, as long as they operate in a professional environment and observe their *hijab* and lawful Islamic gender boundaries. Inappropriate interaction such as joking or flirting with men, however, must be avoided. Engaging in non-work related activities should also be avoided.

Muslim women must also observe proper Islamic attire—they should refrain from wearing anything provocative or that draws negative attention. Islam wants women to command respect by drawing attention to their intellectual capabilities, not their physical appearance.

Islamic history has many examples of women who were active in society, government or politics. Prophet Muhammad's (ṣ) own daughter, Lady Fatima (a), assumed an active role in Muslim society. Her powerful sermons in the Prophet's mosque after his death, coupled with her efforts to rally support for Imam Ali's (a) leadership by visiting the homes of prominent Muslims in Medina, are all a testimony to her active public role.

Lady Fatima's (a) daughter, Lady Zaynab (a), was also well known for her role in spreading the message of her brother Imam al-Husayn (a) after the tragedy of Karbala. She courageously exposed the despotic ruler Yazid for his heinous crimes against the family of the Prophet.

85. Why do Muslim women usually wear *hijab* (head scarf)?

Modesty is incumbent upon both Muslim men and women, but since men and women have been created physically different, the way their modesty is upheld is also different. The Arabic word *hijab* may be translated as "covering" or "concealing." *Hijab* for women covers the entire body save the hands and face. Muslim women don their *hijab* only in public or before men outside of their immediate family. They do not need to wear it in front of other women, their husbands, and certain relatives such as their children, fathers, brothers, uncles, nephews, fathers-in-law, or sons-in-law.

Women living at the time of Prophet Muhammad (ṣ) wore a specific style of *hijab* to adhere to the Qur'anic verses and sayings of the Prophet promoting modesty and chastity. Several verses in the Qur'an speak about modest covering for women, such as chapter 24, verse 31:

> And say to the believing women that they cast down their looks and guard their private parts and do not display their ornaments except what appears thereof, and let them wear their head-coverings over their bosoms.

The passages are not unlike those given in the Bible, which expresses many of the same views on morality as the Qur'an. First Corinthians, chapter 11, verses 4-6 reads: "Every man praying or prophesying, having *his* head covered, dishonoureth his head. But every woman that prayeth or prophesieth with *her* head uncovered dishonoureth her head: for that is even all one as if she were shaven."

Muslims and non-Muslims alike recognize that women are symbols of attraction and temptation in society. Whether in liberal societies or conservative ones, women are viewed differently from men. Even in the United States, women are not permitted to go topless as a man might because to do so is considered distracting and immodest. No one says that this infringes upon women's rights. Muslims believe in increased modesty for women, such that they expand the area that is necessary to be covered; and this also emphasizes upon a woman's inner beauty over her physical beauty.

I think this appreciation for a woman's intrinsic worth is an attitude that many feminists would support, but in the United States many seem to equate the wearing of very revealing attire with liberation and a head covering with oppression. Women's groups in the West have spoken out loudly and clearly about violations of women's rights in Afghanistan, Saudi Arabia, and Iran, but they fell silent when France forced hundreds of thousands of Muslim girls and women to remove their *hijab* in schools and public areas. In addition to infringing upon freedom of worship, the policy forced females to choose between their religion and their education. German legislators and courts have wrestled with similar legislation for public school teachers. For decades, Turkey has imposed a ban on the *hijab* for women who work in the public sector; even those women who observe the *hijab* outside of their work are discriminated against and highly at risk of losing their jobs. I confess bewilderment as to why women's groups eagerly defend Muslim women's rights in Kabul, Riyadh and Tehran, but not in Paris, Berlin and Istanbul?!

Unfortunately, here in the United States, our society tends to deny the silent oppression that is done to women. Our society has become highly sexualized, and women, especially in popular culture, are often regarded as sexual objects. The percentage of women who are harassed in the workplace is staggeringly high. Yet our society overlooks these problems and believes that women in the West are truly liberated. By prescribing the *hijab*, Islam aims at liberating women from this type of injustice. Islam refuses to allow women to be reduced to an object, and it aims for women to be respected and treated with full dignity. The *hijab* is a constant reminder that society must direct its attention to women's intellectual capacities, not their physical bodies.

The beauty of *hijab* is that it establishes a standard for women independent from the standard of men. If we actually analyze the status of women in many western societies, we realize that they essentially accept men as the standard, and women are constantly compared to men. If men do not cover their hair, women should not; if men wear jeans, so should women; if men spend more time at work and less time at home raising children, then women should do the same; if men join the military, so should women. This is not to say that women should not participate in these activities, but the point is that our society teaches that women should do these things just because men do—in order to compete with them. This essentially makes everything feminine inferior and everything masculine superior. But Islam has created an independent standard for women and this standard is not based on men. It is a standard that has been created by God, and although this standard is different than the standard of men, it is equal.

Islamic scholars disagree somewhat about the specific requirements of *hijab*. Muslim women wear many varieties of modest clothing, and there is a range in the amount of coverage these clothes provide. In certain very conservative areas, women will wear a *hijab* that covers the entire body, including the face, but even conservative Saudi Arabia does not require the face veil. In the majority of the Muslim world, it is safe to say that women wear their *hijab* voluntarily and proudly, declaring not their subjugation to men, but rather their submission to God.

86. Is it okay to wear *hijab* even if one does not understand the importance or rationale behind it?

God will not punish a woman for wearing *hijab* even though she may not be convinced about its purpose. On the other hand, God may not fully reward a woman for wearing it if she is not convinced about its purpose. If a woman wears it out of conviction, submission, and dedication, then God will reward her greatly for every second that she wears it. To be rewarded, one must wear the *hijab* for the sake of God, not one's parents, friends, or society.

Remember that God is our creator, and He is all the Most-wise and knows what is best for us. If He has mandated or decreed something for us, then know for sure that it is for our own good, and we must submit to whatever God has ordained. Prophet Muhammad (ṣ) once said:

O People! You are like patients and God is the physician. Whatever is good for the patient rests in what the physician prescribes, not in what the patient desires. [216]

God does not benefit from our obeying Him or our doing good actions; rather, it is we who benefit from following His commands. He only looks out for our best interests. Thus, we must always submit to whatever God has mandated.

87. Do women have to wear socks and cover their feet as a part of Islamic *hijab*?

According to the majority of Muslim scholars, once a woman is in public areas where she can be seen by men, (other than immediate relatives such as her father, husband, or brother), then she must cover her entire body with the exception of her face and hands up to the wrists. This includes covering the feet as well. However, it does not necessarily require one to wear socks—shoes, a long dress, or any other covering garment or object could cover them. But if a woman is not wearing shoes and is not wearing a dress that stretches all the way to her feet, then opaque socks may be the best option. Keep in mind that they cannot be revealing or transparent, such as nylons.

88. Can a woman's ears be showing when wearing *hijab*?

A woman's ears must be covered in *hijab*. The only parts allowed to be shown are the roundness of the face and the hands up to the wrist.

---

[216] *Mustadrak al-Wasa'el*, vol. 3, p. 177

89. Is it acceptable for women to play sports?

Women may enjoy and compete in sports and activities when they are among other women. When men are spectators, however, it may pose a dilemma since the mandated Islamic covering (*hijab*) must be observed, and depending on the style of the sport, it may require women to compromise their physical posture. Either way, playing sports for women is permissible as long as it does not compromise their modesty and *hijab*.

It must be remembered that *hijab* is not simply a headscarf that covers the hair, but rather *hijab* signifies modesty in clothing, behavior, posture and all types of interaction with the opposite gender.

90. Are Muslim women allowed to drive?

There is no Islamic prohibition for a Muslim woman to drive. Muslim women are encouraged to pursue their education, are allowed to work, travel and do anything that does not compromise their modesty or *hijab*.

Muslim women in the United States and in Muslim countries are permitted to drive a car and operate a vehicle. The only exception is Saudi Arabia, which bans women from driving. However, this ban has no Islamic basis whatsoever; it is simply based on Saudi culture and social norms. Contrary to what some westerners believe, it does not represent Islam's position on women driving. The society of Saudi Arabia is known for its rigidity and unfavorable stance towards women. Their norms do not represent the norms of the Muslim world, and in certain aspects they do not necessarily represent the rulings of Islam.

91. Can a Muslim woman get a back massage from another woman?

A massage between women is not prohibited (*haram*). However, any such act that, God forbid, provokes ill intentions between two people will become problematic and is ultimately not permissible. As long as the massage takes place in a totally intimate-free, normal frame of work, then it is permissible.

However, certain limitations still need to be observed. For instance, a massage should not extend beyond the normal boundaries, meaning a masseuse cannot look at the recipient's private areas. As well, giving a massage does not justify becoming naked and exposing one's private parts (the genitals). Furthermore, the massage cannot be sexual in nature. These characteristics would make the massage, even if given by one woman to another, not permissible in Islam.

92. Is it permissible for a Muslim woman to show her hair to a co-worker who claims to be a lesbian?

There are a few narrations that indicate it is not recommended for a Muslim woman to expose her beauty before other non-religious, non-Muslim women. The reason is that these women may describe a Muslim woman to other men. Since they are not religious, they may not understand that the privacy of a woman's beauty can only be viewed by a few select individuals. In this case, we cannot absolutely say that this Muslim woman cannot show her hair to a lesbian. However, if there is a possibility that exposing her hair to a person could be a temptation for the lesbian and encourage prohibited acts, then it is best that she does not do so. She should try to keep her interaction which such people to a minimum, and restrict it only to the format of business at work.

93. Can women wear nail polish on their hands while performing their prayers?

Women can wear fingernail polish while praying, but they must remove the nail polish before performing ablution (*wudhu*) before the prayers. Water must reach all parts of the ablution area, and anything such as nail polish will be a barrier which prevents water from reaching those parts. If a woman wishes to paint her nails between ablution and the prayers, that is fine. For the next ablution, however, she will have to remove the polish again.

94. Is it forbidden for a woman to enter a Masjid (mosque) during her monthly cycle?

A woman is prohibited from entering any Masjid (mosque), meaning the actual sanctuary area where the prayers are performed, during her monthly cycle. The courtyards, hallways, or corridors surrounding the mosque are not included in this definition. A woman can be in any of these areas during her monthly cycle.

Likewise, a person in a state of *janabah*—someone who has entered into a state of spiritual impurity due to sexual relations or the ejaculation of sperm and has not performed the ceremonial shower (*ghusl*)—is not permitted to enter a Masjid, but may enter adjacent courtyards, hallways, and corridors.

Marriage

95. If a Muslim does not get married, then is that person's faith not complete?

There are many narrations from the Prophet and the Imams emphasizing the significance of marriage in Islam. One narration from Prophet Muhammad (ṣ) says: "He who gets married fulfills half of his faith (by getting married), so he should fear God in the other half."[217] This narration shows the symbolic significance of marriage: protecting one's chastity, protecting oneself from falling into the pit of sexual promiscuity, and in continuing the future generations.

One major danger of humanity is sexual desire, and getting married is one way of sublimating this dangerous lure or attraction. Single men and women are at greater risk of sexual promiscuity. Hence, the narration from the Prophet says: "The worst of our dead ones are those who died single."[218] This means that people who are single, by leading a single life and not yet morally securing a major need, may be at risk of committing a great sin, such as adultery.

Since Islam considers any extramarital relations between men and women a sin, marriage is the only arrangement in which a Muslim individual can fulfill his or her sexual desires.

---

[217] *Al-Kafi*, vol. 5, p. 329

[218] *Bihar al-Anwar*, vol. 100, p. 220

The sexual drive is one of the most powerful human instincts, if not the most powerful, so Islam promotes early marriage. Often some individuals without the necessary means to get married turn to unlawful or illicit alternatives such as pursuing prostitutes, watching pornography, or indulging in other immoral sexual acts. Marriage, therefore, seems to be the best remedy to all of these undesirable outcomes.

96. What does Islam say about interfaith marriages?

Islam permits a Muslim man to marry a non-Muslim woman only if she is of the People of the Book: a Christian or a Jew. A Muslim man is not allowed to marry a follower of other religions or an atheist.

Islam highly encourages Muslim husbands to help their non-Muslim wives to learn about Islam and ultimately convert. Having two faiths at home can be a major source of confusion for children, and often those children whose parents follow different religions suffer a loss of identity.

On Fridays, they may feel like they are Muslims; on Sundays, they may tend to be Christians. One must assess the consequences such upbringing can have on the future generations. This may cause the children to become liars and hypocrites—when they are with their Muslim father, they will pretend to be like him, Muslim; but when they are with their mother, they will pretend to be like her, Christian.

Therefore, even though Islam permits such marriages (a Muslim male marrying a Christian or Jewish female), Islam does not encourage it due to the potentially detrimental consequences of such a marriage. The best solution is to encourage the wife to convert to Islam. Here, the word *encourage* needs to be emphasized, because a man cannot force his non-Muslim wife to convert. Islam does not believe in force or coercion in these matters.

> There is no compulsion in religion; truly the right way has become clearly distinct from error; therefore, whoever disbelieves in the Devil and believes in God he indeed has laid hold on the firmest handle, which shall not break off, and God is Hearing, Knowing.[219]

If a person converts to Islam but does not have a strong conviction, then this conversion will be rendered irrelevant and fruitless. Encouraging a non-Muslim wife is best done by setting a good and decent example on how a Muslim should act. Honesty, integrity, kindness, respect, and humbleness are qualities that are highly encouraged by Islam and extremely attractive to others.

When Prophet Muhammad (ṣ) dispatched Imam Ali (a) to Yemen, he summoned him to come back and told him:

> O Ali, do not fight them before you invite them to Islam [and they begin to attack you]. I swear by the One who sent me as a Prophet, if God guides one individual through you it is better for you than if you own everything that the sun shines upon.[220]

However, when dealing with a female Muslim desiring to marry a non-Muslim male, Islam takes a harder line. Islam does not permit a female Muslim to marry a non-Muslim male, not because of any prejudice or to promote male superiority, but to protect the future

---

[219] *Noble Qur'an*, Suratul Baqarah (2), verse 256
[220] *Al-Kafi*, vol. 5, p. 28

of any children who may come from this marriage. In most countries, the children of divorced couples go to the husband. In the case above, this literally means that the custody of the Muslim children would go to a non-Muslim, who might very well convert them to another religion. Islam considers it the responsibility of Muslim fathers and mothers to protect their children's Islamic identity by all means.

97. My adult daughter wants to marry a non-Muslim. He believes in God but was brought up following "no religion." My daughter has read that we are "all born Muslims" but parents and society change some people. She is asking us, "Is this man more Muslim than not?" How do I respond?

There is a narration from Prophet Muhammad (ṣ) that states everyone is born a Muslim but the parents change one's religion.[221] This however does not prove that everyone is a Muslim. To remain a Muslim (or to return to Islam), one must witness that there is no god but God and that Muhammad (ṣ) is His messenger.

If the man your daughter wishes to marry witnesses and believes in these two statements, then he is a Muslim. If not, then he is not a Muslim, and thus she cannot marry him.

98. Is there a reason that a man can marry four women and not just two?

First, a point of emphasis: norms and traditions vary from one nation to another and from one culture to another. Things that may be considered unacceptable in one society may be considered acceptable in other societies.

---

[221] *Man la Yahdharahul Faqih*, vol. 2, p. 49

In the United States, it is considered a crime for a thirteen-year-old girl to marry a nineteen-year-old man. It can even be called statutory rape, and it may result in imprisonment of the husband. However, this kind of a marriage is common in many countries around the world, such as in India, Pakistan, Yemen, the Persian Gulf countries, and others. It is normal and legal, and many people do not see anything wrong with it. (In many European countries and some U.S. states, a girl may get married at the age of fifteen or sixteen with parental consent).

Similarly, a marriage between two gay men might be considered legal in certain U.S. states, but it is illegal and punishable in many countries of the world.

Also in the U.S., more and more eighth and ninth graders are losing their virginity these days, and while American society overlooks such trends, many parts of the world treat them much more seriously. Thus, social norms are not black and white and depend on the society in which one lives.

Polygamy was widely practiced in pre-Islamic times, with no limit on the number of wives a man could have. One main incentive behind polygamy in tribal societies, which lacked civil governments, was to have as many children as possible to protect the legacy of the family and the tribe at large. Another was that, for farmers, polygamy was a way to have more help on the farm. Thus, many Arab men tended to have many wives.

Islam restricted polygamy to a maximum of four wives but did not revoke it. The reason it did not revoke it is because the social system at the time heavily depended upon polygamy. Had it insisted on monogamy, Islam would have shocked a society that heavily depended upon more than one wife. Instead, Islam took gradual steps to restrict this practice and declared a limit of four simultaneous wives.

People today may think of four as a large number, but at the time of Islam's inception, many men were demanding a lot more. Imagine the pressure that mounted on Prophet Muhammad (ṣ) when he limited men who were used to having an unlimited number of wives to only four.

Islam does not encourage, under normal circumstances, to have more than one wife at a time. In fact, according to some scholars, it is not even recommended. However, if a situation arises in which having more than one wife becomes necessary—for example, if his first wife incurs a sickness that impedes her from her marital responsibility—then a man may want to marry an additional woman. In doing so, the man must exercise complete equity among his wives and not favor one over another. This is very difficult for many men to do and makes polygamy quite difficult for most men to practice.

The Prophet was an exception because he was not motivated in the same manner as most human beings, in pursuit of personal pleasure, and he was the only one permitted to have more than four wives.

A husband is obligated to obtain his first wife's permission for a second wife in only two cases:

1. If he is marrying a non-Muslim
2. If his wife stipulated her consent in the prenuptial agreement of their Islamic marriage contract on the day of their Islamic engagement

If any of these two conditions exists, then he cannot marry another woman without her permission.

99. Does a female Muslim convert need to obtain permission from her non-Muslim parents to marry a Muslim man?

A woman who has converted to Islam does not need the permission of her non-Muslim parents in order to get married. Only a virgin Muslim woman requires her father's permission to marry a man. Many scholars state that if a Muslim woman is responsible, financially independent and not living with her father, then she does not require his permission for marriage.

Family Matters

100. Why is "adoption" not recommended in Islam, but caring for an orphan is regarded as being important? What is the difference?

The reasons that Islam may not allow legal adoption are the following:

1. Adoption requires a change of identity for an adopted person; and this is not permissible in Islam. Changing identity requires that we not attribute the adopted child to his biological parents, but rather to the adoptive parents, which is a misleading falsehood.

2. Changing the identity would entitle individuals to inherit from people whom they are not otherwise entitled to inherit from. The laws of inheritance are based on a biological relationship. If we assume that the adopted son is equal to a biological son, then this will require that we follow these laws. The adopted son would be entitled to inheritance, thus depriving the other heirs of some of their rightful share of an inheritance.

3. Adoption has the potential to violate the rules (known as *mahramiyya*) about which women a man can see without their headscarf. A man can see the following women without their Islamic head covering (*hijab*) because he is an immediate male relative (*mahram*): wife, daughter, step-daughter, sisters, niece, granddaughter, mother, grandmother, and mother-in-law.

If a girl is an adopted daughter, she does not qualify to be *mahram* with the man who adopted her when she reaches puberty. He cannot see her without *hijab*, nor can he have any sort of physical contact—such as hugging or shaking hands with her. Adoption, by changing her identity, would make it as though they are *mahram*, but the laws are based on biological association, and an adopted child would not in fact be *mahram*. For these reasons, adoption is not permitted.

However, if adoption is conducted in such a way that there is not a legal change of identity, nor entail any of the above-mentioned issues, then it is okay to adopt a child.

Imam Ali (a) had an adopted son who was also his stepson. That son was Muhammad, the son of Abu Bakr. He was only two when his father died, and Imam Ali (a) married his mother. Imam Ali (a) used to say Muhammad is my son from the offspring of Abu Bakr. But the Imam never changed his identity; something that can cause the previously mentioned problems.

Muslims are highly encouraged to care for orphans, bring them into their homes, care for them, and raise them as one of their own. We have copious narrations from the Prophet and his family that highly encourage us to tend to the needs of the orphans. One narration promises a special place in paradise for those who bring joy to an orphan.[222] Another narration from Prophet Muhammad (s) tells us that the one who takes care of an orphan will be with the Prophet in heaven.[223]

However, while we are encouraged to care for them, we are not permitted to change their identities; and orphans are not entitled to inheritance from their foster parents; nor can the parents

---

[222] *Mizan al-Hikma*, vol. 4, p. 3708

[223] *Ibid.*

inherit from their wealth, and orphans are not *mahram* to their adoptive parents either.

101. Is it prohibited for a step-father to see his step-daughter without the Islamic headscarf (*hijab*)?

Before we answer the question, let us review what God says in the Noble Qur'an in this regard:

> Forbidden to you [for marriage] are your mothers and your daughters and your sisters and your paternal aunts and your maternal aunts, and brothers' daughters and sisters' daughters and your mothers that have suckled you and your foster-sisters and mothers of your wives and your step-daughters who are in your guardianship, (born) of your wives to whom you have gone in, but if you have not gone in to them, there is no blame on you (in marrying them), and the wives of your sons who are of your own loins and that you should have two sisters together, except what has already passed; surely God is Forgiving, Merciful.[224]

In this verse, God mentions the women that a Muslim man cannot marry and thus can see without *hijab* (known as *maharim* - the plural of *mahram*).

One of them is a step-daughter after the marriage to her mother is consummated. In this case, it is also permanently prohibited (*haram*) for a step-father to marry his step-daughter.

According to this verse, girls can see their step-fathers and talk to them without *hijab*. Shaking their hand and hugging them is also permissible.

---

[224] *Noble Qur'an*, Suratul Nisa (4), verse 23

102. How should parents deal with a disobedient child?

God tells us in the Qur'an about a disobedient son and a righteous father: Noah (a) and his son. Noah (a) was a responsible father who did everything possible to keep his son on the straight path, but his wife, who was not Muslim (meaning a believer in Noah's message), and their lax society, helped lead the son down the path of corruption.

What we learn from this story is that even a child with an excellent parent may go astray. This is especially true if one of the parents is not as righteous as the other. This does not absolve parents from attempting to guide their children down the right path. It does make it more difficult, however.

First, and perhaps the best advice for parents with a rebellious or disobedient child, is not to give up on him or her. Keep advising and trying your best to correct the behavior, keeping in mind that God will definitely hold parents responsible for how they deal with their kids. The Qur'an says:

> O you who believe! save yourselves and your families from a fire whose fuel is men and stones; over it are angels stern and strong, they do not disobey God in what He commands them, and do as they are commanded.[225]

This verse indicates that parents have a great responsibility towards their children. It is their obligation to teach them to follow the path of Islam and the commandments of God.

In this regard, Imam Hasan (a) says: "I wonder at someone who avoids consuming unhealthy food into his stomach, how he would

---

[225] *Noble Qur'an*, Suratul Tahrim (66), verse 6

not avoid putting damaging food into his mind."[226] This is applicable to the food that you feed your child's body and mind as well, as parents are responsible for its content.

Second, parents should not be too accommodating or lenient; and this is especially true for teenagers. Parents are responsible for checking on their teenagers and knowing where they spend their time, who they associate with, and what they are doing. They should help them select good friends and should not give them unlimited freedom, because this can corrupt them. Unrestricted freedom while at the same time providing for all of their material needs, will prove fatal to the well-being of children. A rebellious child who chooses to defy his or her religious limits should not see a welcoming face from his or her father or mother. Parents should make it clear that they are not happy about the choices that their child is making. They should not accept what a child has done if it transcends the limits of Islam.

Third, both parents should have a unified position with their children. A child should not find lenience with his mother and a tough stance with his father or vice versa. Both parents need to be consistent in their discipline. Often this entails discussing ahead of time what measures will be taken if a child transgresses the limits.

Finally, if parents see that their rebellious child is showing signs of rehabilitation or change, they should immediately welcome that by encouraging them to continue on the path of reform. In some cases, the stubbornness of parents and their inflexibility may discourage rebellious children from changing

---

[226] *Bihar al-Anwar*, vol. 1, p. 218

their way when that may otherwise be inclined to change for the better.

103. What does Islam say about making use of sperm donation for couples who are infertile and cannot conceive?

Islam is the religion of mercy and affection, and therefore it understands that each married man and woman would like to fulfill the instincts of motherhood and fatherhood within them.

However, in doing so, one must use moral and ethical means. The end does not always justify the means. Artificial inseminations are permitted only under strict conditions in which the donor of the sperm is permissible (*halal*) to the woman who is to be inseminated. In other words, it must be her own husband—either her permanent husband or her temporary husband.

If a woman enters into a temporary marriage in order to acquire sperm from that temporary husband (by first divorcing her first husband and then maintaining her 'waiting period' after divorce) and then remarries her permanent husband, the permanent husband may raise the child. However, the child will in fact belong to the donor of the sperm—her temporary husband. The child will therefore carry the name of the temporary husband, and the laws of inheritance will be applicable only between the child and the temporary husband (who is the real biological father) not the permanent husband.

104. A person is "certain" that he is a homosexual and is in a state of confusion in this regard. Is this completely against Islam? Should he take it as a challenge from God?

God has created us and He knows best what benefits us and what harms us. The limits He has placed for us are to help us lead a blessed and prosperous life that will bring us closer to Him, elevate our spirituality, and prepare us for the hereafter. God's limits and laws also serve to test us, as we have been created to be tested.

Homosexuality may indeed be a challenge from God. Some people are tested with their health, some with their wealth, some with their family, some with their careers, etc..., and some people may be tested with homosexuality. One must struggle against his desires and urges to overcome this test. If one sacrifices his desires and passes this test, then God will reward this person in ways which cannot even be imagined.

Having involuntary homosexual urges is not a sin; but acting upon them by engaging in homosexual behavior is a grave sin. God will not punish a person for something which is beyond one's control (i.e. the presence of these urges), but God will hold people accountable for their actions.

Islam is completely against practicing homosexuality, and it is a condition that must be treated. Just as alcoholics, pedophiles and those who have incestuous urges need to seek treatment, homosexuals also should seek professional assistance.

Here are several steps that might prove helpful in overcoming homosexuality:

1. Sincerely seek assistance from God so that He may rid you from this condition. Constantly pray for help and assistance from Him.

2. Seek therapy or professional help so that these urges and thoughts are expelled from your mind.

3. We all have emotional needs and require love. When we say that those with homosexual tendencies should not engage in same-sex relationships, we are not saying that they do not have a chance at loving others and being loved. They can fulfill these needs by emotionally investing more in their parents, siblings, children (if they have), other family members or friends (but obviously not in a sexual manner). While this may not completely fulfill their needs, it may significantly help them.

4. Get married with the opposite sex, and allow God to help you gradually bond with your spouse. God will indeed deliver affection and mercy to your marital life. Marriage will also fulfill your physical needs to an extent. While homosexuals may not find themselves attracted to the opposite sex, they may still meet their physical needs with them.

5. Never give up. Even if these urges continue for years, take this as an ongoing challenge or test. Keep in mind that God will highly reward you for all of the difficulties you will experience throughout this time.

6. Try to avoid being around homosexual friends, and do not attend homosexual gatherings and parties.

7. Read the Holy Qur'an on a daily basis.

8. Believe that change is possible. Do not convince yourself that you will never be able to change. While change is undoubtedly difficult, it is possible, eventually.

Rites of Worship

105. Other than the five daily prayers, what are the other mandatory prayers?

Other mandatory prayers include:

1. **The funeral prayer (*Salat al-Janaza*):** This prayer is performed after a deceased Muslim is ceremoniously washed and wrapped in the white burial shroud, but before the actual burial.

It requires a minimum of one Muslim to perform the prayer. This minimum requirement is called voluntary binding (*al-Wajib al-Kifa'i*), which means that when a Muslim individual dies, there should be at least one Muslim volunteer to perform the funeral prayer on him or her. If a minimum of one Muslim performs this obligation, then it is not required by other Muslims to perform it. It is only recommended for other people to join. But if no Muslim chooses to perform this prayer on the deceased, then all of the Muslims are deemed sinful in the eyes of God. So initially, it is mandatory for everyone to pray, but once one person volunteers, then it becomes recommended for others to join (but it is not compulsory on them).

The funeral prayer consists of five statements of "God is Greatest" (*takbeerats*) with a short supplication (*du'a*) between each *takbeer*. The prayer starts with a *takbeer*, then in the first supplication, the person leading the prayer and also those taking part in this prayer read the two declarations that there is no god but Allah and Muhammad (ṣ) is His messenger. After the second takbeer, the people send blessings upon Prophet Muhammad (ṣ) and his family. After the third takbeer, one asks God to forgive all of the believers and Muslims. After the fourth takbeer, one prays for the deceased and asks God to forgive him or her. The prayer ends with the fifth takbeer.

The funeral prayer is performed while standing and there is no bowing or prostration in this prayer. Also, this prayer does not require an ablution, nor for one to be in a state of spiritual purity.

2. The signs prayer (Salat al-Ayat): This becomes mandatory at the time of an earthquake or a solar or lunar eclipse; and it consists of two units (rak'at).

In the first unit, after reciting the opening chapter of Al-Fatiha, a short chapter of five verses or more, including Bismillah as a verse, should be recited, such as Surah al-Ikhlas, chapter 112 of the Qur'an. After each verse the praying individual bows down (for the ruku). If the chapter chosen has more than five verses, then that chapter should be divided into five parts. After each part, the person performing this prayer will bow down for ruku. After the fifth ruku, one stands and then performs the two prostrations (sujood). Then one performs the second unit exactly like the first unit.

However, it is not mandatory to recite the same chapter in the second unit as was recited in the first unit. A different chapter of five verses or more can be used.

After the second prostration in the second unit, the prayer will end with the testimony (tashahud) and salutation (tasleem).

An alternative method of performing the signs prayer is to recite Al-Fatiha and a whole chapter before each ruku, thereby reciting Al-Fatiha and any other chapter five times in each unit.

When the signs prayer is necessary because of an earthquake, then the person must pray as soon as possible. However, for a solar or lunar eclipse, a Muslim must rush to pray it before the eclipse is over. If one misses it, then it must be made up afterward unless it was a partial solar eclipse and the person was not aware of the eclipse while it occurred.

The signs prayer is not required for eclipses not visible in one's area or for earthquakes too far away or too subtle to notice. An earthquake has to be powerful enough that at least a few people feel the tremors. If it is only recorded at geological centers, then the signs prayer is not obligatory for one to recite.

The signs prayer is required only for earthquakes and eclipses. Floods, avalanches, volcanoes, blizzards, and other naturally occurring phenomena do not necessitate the prayer, although it is recommended to perform it.

3. The Festival prayer (*Salat al-'Eid*): There are two Festival prayers – one marking the end of the month of Ramadhan (the month of fasting) and the other to celebrate the completion of the *hajj*. Both of these become mandatory at the time of the advent of Imam al-Mahdi (a). During his occultation, their performance is highly recommended.

4. The Friday prayers (*Salat al-Jumu'ah*): At the time of Prophet Muhammad (ṣ), Friday prayer was mandatory upon all Muslim men. In our time, most scholars state that it is not mandatory to perform it. Some scholars say that if one chooses to attend the

Friday prayer then it becomes mandatory in the sense that it substitutes for the noon (*Dhuhr*) prayer. At the time of the advent of Imam al-Mahdi (a), it will once again become mandatory upon all to perform it.

5. Prayer of circumambulation (*Salat al-Tawaaf*): Muslims who perform *umrah* or *hajj* circumambulate the Ka'bah seven times. Upon finishing, they must perform a prayer of two units behind the standing place of Prophet Abraham (a). This prayer is mandatory and is called the prayer of circumambulation, and it is performed just like the morning prayer.

6. Personal obligatory prayers: If someone pledges to God to conduct a certain prayer, then this prayer becomes obligatory due to the pledge made. For example, someone pledges to God that if he passes an exam, then he will perform two units of prayer. If this person passes the exam, he must perform a two unit prayer.

106. When is the proper time to pray the midnight prayer (*Salat al-Layl*)?

The midnight prayer is made up of eleven units and should be performed between midnight and dawn. The closer to dawn that one performs it, the better it is.

The period that immediately precedes dawn is called *sahar*. Many narrations state that this period is highly blessed. The gates of God's mercy are wide open, and it is the best time to turn to God, repent and supplicate.

"Midnight" is not officially defined as 12 a.m. Islamically, it is the midpoint between the evening and morning prayers. For example, if the evening prayer is at 5:30 p.m. and the morning prayer is at 6 a.m., then the midpoint is 11:45 p.m. Thus, "midnight" varies from day to day, from region to region and from winter to summer based on the evening and morning prayer times.

107. Can we perform the midnight prayer (*Salat al-Layl*) if we still have required prayers to make up from the past?

Owing missed prayers does not bar someone from performing the midnight prayer (*Salat al-Layl*). One can still pray the midnight prayers.

The same thing cannot be said for fasting, however. If someone has a certain number of obligatory fasts to be made up, then according to Muslim scholars, one cannot perform recommended (*mustahab*) fasts before fulfilling those missed fasts.[255]

In addition, Muslim scholars believe that if someone is obligated to perform the *hajj*, then one must perform *hajj* for oneself before performing *hajj* on behalf of another person.

108. How do you make your intention for recommended prayers?

Simply keep three things in mind when making the intention:

1. This prayer is a recommended/extra prayer (as opposed to a mandatory prayer).

2. Specify which prayer it is (e.g., *Nafilah al-Subh* – the recommended prayer of the morning).

---

[255] According to Ayatollah Sistani. This can be found in his English translation of Islamic rulings, ruling no. 1572.

3. State that you are praying to seek closeness to God.

109. Can you elaborate on the recommended additional prayers, what to say at the beginning of each prayer, and why they are beneficial?

The recommended additional daily prayers are known in Arabic as the *"Nawafil al-Yawmiyya,"* which means "the daily extra prayers." There are thirty-four units (*rak'at*) of prayer which are highly recommended for a Muslim individual to perform every day. Imam Hasan al-Askari (a), the eleventh Imam of Ahlul Bayt, states that praying them is among the signs of a believer.[256]

The additional recommended prayers are as follows:

1. *Nafilah al-Subh*: one two-unit prayer to be recited before the morning prayer.

2. *Nafilah al-Dhuhr*: four two-unit prayers to be recited before the noon prayer.

3. *Nafilah al-Asr*: four two-unit prayers to be recited before the afternoon prayer.

4. *Nafilah al-Maghrib*: two two-unit prayers to be recited after the evening prayer.

5. *Nafilah al-Isha*: one two-unit prayer, to be recited while sitting, after the night prayer (the two units sitting down are equivalent to one unit standing).

6. *Nafilah al-Layl*: four two-unit prayers to be recited after midnight but before dawn.

---

[256] *Misbah al-Mutahajjid*, p. 788, first edition

7. *Salat al-Shaf*: one two-unit prayer to be recited after the eight units of *Nafilah al-Layl*.

8. *Salat al-Witr*: one prayer of only one unit to be recited after *Nafilah al-Shaf*.

The last three prayers, which total eleven units, are collectively called the midnight prayers or *Salat al-Layl*.

The total is thirty-four units of recommended prayers, which is double the seventeen units of the five mandatory daily prayers. The total of both the mandatory and recommended prayers is fifty-one units.

Some narrations state that these extra thirty-four units are for us to pray to compensate for any shortcomings we may have had with the seventeen mandatory units.[257] In other words, the thirty-four units complete the five daily prayers and "fix" them if we have not performed them in the best possible manner.

According to some narrations, a Muslim individual who performs these fifty-one units each day achieves a high level of faith (*imaan*) and belief. There is a *Hadith al-Qudsi*[258] by God that

---

[257] *Al-Kafi*, vol. 3, p. 363

[258] Of course, everything that Prophet Muhammad (ṣ) taught us was from God. Usually the Prophet (ṣ) taught us Islam through his words and composition. In other words, he paraphrased what God had revealed to him. However, sometimes the Prophet conveyed to us the message of God verbatim, word for word. The clearest example of this was the Noble Qur'an, which is the exact word of God, not the Prophet only conveying the meaning of what God revealed to him. Sometimes, the Prophet conveyed to us the message of God word for word, without paraphrasing, but he indicated that this was not part of the Qur'an. Such sayings by the

states: "My beloved servant continues to seek closeness to me by performing mandatory and recommended prayers, so much so that I will love him, and whoever I love I become his eyes through which he sees, his ears through which he hears, and his hands which he moves."[259] This means that a person who performs many prayers sincerely will achieve such a high level of faith that it is as if God is manifested through all of one's actions. This is because a faithful person dedicates everything to God and strictly obeys Him. In every action, that believer will represent the genuine teachings of God.

When one wants to perform the extra prayers, one makes an intention with the name of the prayer as given earlier (e.g., *Nafilah al-Dhuhr*), and the number of units you intend to perform. Then you need to recite *Surah al-Fatiha* and another complete *surah* in every unit. Note that these extra prayers are valid if one does not recite another *surah* after *Surah al-Fatiha* in every unit, but it is highly recommended for one to recite another chapter.

Essentially, each additional two-unit prayer is performed exactly like the morning prayer, only changing the intention with the name of the prayer to be performed. Only in the last three units of the midnight prayer (*al-Shaf* and *al-Witr*) there is a slight difference because there are certain chapters of the Qur'an and supplications that are recommended to be recited. One can refer to the books of supplication for their details. There are many other recommended prayers that can be performed on a daily basis, a

---

Prophet are called *Hadith Al-Qudsi*, which means "sacred or divine saying."

[259] *Kanz al-Ummal*, vol. 1, p. 230, hadith no. 1157

monthly basis, or on important Islamic occasions. Many of these extra prayers carry amazingly high rewards and benefits.

110. What is the best way to remain focused during the prayers?

One of the most challenging tasks for Muslims is to concentrate during their prayers. According to many narrations, the Devil attempts to distract people a lot during the prayer and causes them to lose their focus and attention. It is for this reason that the place where a worshipper stands for prayer is called in Arabic the *mihrab* - which means a battleground or a place of fighting. When we commence our prayers, we are constantly fighting the Devil, who strives to divert our attention and devalue our prayers. Prayer is a manifestation of the internal struggle that we all have to go through in order to seek closeness to God.

In the Qur'an God forewarned individuals who do not concentrate on their prayers:

So woe to the praying ones, Who are unmindful of their prayers.[260]

Here are a few tips that might be helpful for an individual who wishes to focus better during the prayers:

1. Before going to pray, attempt to detach yourself completely from this world. Turn all cell phones off and stay away from any distractive elements such as the television, a radio, or noisy rooms.

2. Use the bathroom beforehand.

---

[260] *Noble Qur'an*, Suratul Ma'oun (107), verses 4–5

3. Do not pray in busy, noisy environments, such as busy public places.

4. If running a business, try to solve business problems prior to engaging in prayers. This will help keep the mind clear from distractions.

5. If you are the mother of a young baby, try to put your baby to sleep before you engage in prayers so the child will not be a distraction.

6. Start your prayers by reciting: "*Audhu billahi min al-shaytanir rajeem*," which means, "I seek refuge with God from the accursed Devil." God says in the Qur'an:

So when you recite the Qur'an, then seek refuge with God from the accursed Devil.[261]

7. When you are praying, take your time and perform all of the actions of prayer (e.g., bowing and prostrating) properly and thoroughly, not in a hurried manner. Try to utter the words correctly and with proper pronunciation.

8. Give yourself enough time to complete your prayers before the time for prayer has elapsed. Do not wait until the last few minutes to pray and then create your own distractions by hurrying through your prayers unnecessarily.

9. Contemplate on the meaning of the verses that you are reciting and the actions you are performing. For instance (as it was also pointed out in Question 44), Imam Ali (a)

---

[261] *Noble Qur'an*, Suratul Nahl (16), verse 98

shed light on the meaning of the two prostrations that we perform in every unit. He taught us that when we lower our head to the ground for the first prostration, we are reminding ourselves that we were all created from clay (the ground). Raising our head represents our birth and entry into this life. Lowering our head again upon the earth for the second prostration symbolizes our death and return to the ground. Lifting our head the second time implies the Day of Judgment when we will all be resurrected. Thinking about the symbolism behind such acts will help us remain focused.

One's state of mind will play a major role in how focused a person will be during prayer. An individual should know deep down in one's heart that God is watching everyone while praying. One should realize that one is praying before the Lord of the heavens and the earth. This will definitely give one a sense of serenity, reverence, and submission, which will lead a person to focus more during prayers.

When we have God in our minds with all of His glory and might, then we will exhibit more humility and reverence. Prophet Muhammad (ṣ) said, "When you worship God, act as if you see Him, and know that if you do not see Him, then indeed He definitely sees you."[263]

Citizens in their everyday lives, if they know that a government or group is monitoring them, they will exhibit a higher level of performance. Knowing that God is constantly watching us, especially during our prayers, should make us feel God's holy and

---

[263] *Al-Amali* of Shaykh al-Sadouq, p. 526

majestic presence, and consequently it should help us maintain better focus in our prayers.

111. The Qur'an orders the Muslims to shorten their prayers if someone may attack them. If one is safe to perform prayers in the normal fashion, then does one still have to shorten them when travelling?

In chapter 4, verses 101–103 of the Qur'an say:

> *And when you journey, there is no blame on you if you shorten the prayer, if you fear that those who disbelieve will cause you distress, surely the unbelievers are your open enemy. And when you are among them and keep up the prayer for them, let a party of them stand up with you, and let them take their arms; then when they have prostrated themselves let them go to your rear, and let another party who have not prayed come forward and pray with you, and let them take their precautions and their arms; (for) those who disbelieve desire that you may be careless of your arms and your luggage, so that they may then turn upon you with a sudden united attack, and there is no blame on you, if you are annoyed with rain or if you are sick, that you lay down your arms, and take your precautions; surely God has prepared a disgraceful chastisement for the unbelievers. Then when you have finished the prayer, remember God standing and sitting and reclining; but when you are secure (from danger) keep up prayer; surely prayer is a timed ordinance for the believers.*[264]

---

[264] *Noble Qur'an*, Suratul Nisa (4), verses 101–103

Many narrations that interpret these verses and detail the protocol of prayer indicate that fear of enemies is one of the reasons for shortening the prayer. But there is another reason, and that is the God-given right to seek comfort. In other words, the narrations say that the prayer can be shortened when one has a fear of the enemy or when is traveling. The distance that must be traveled before the rule of the shortened prayer becomes applicable is 22 km (13.7 miles) one way and 44 km (27.3 miles) round trip. If you travel this amount or more, then you **must** shorten your prayer.

God has created a comfort zone for each Muslim in which one should feel comfortable practicing one's faith. Since Islam is the religion of ease and mercy, God wishes to make it easier on a traveler. God has ordained for us to shorten our noon (*dhuhr*), afternoon (*asr*), and night (*isha*) prayers while traveling, as well as not to fast if we are traveling in the month of Ramadhan. Obviously, praying half of the normal prayer is easier for travelers who are often in a rush to keep up with their travel plans and are outside of their normal environment.

112. How should a person pray on an airplane?

When it is time for prayer, a Muslim must perform his or her prayers; and thus, praying on an airplane is as mandatory as praying elsewhere. A few points to consider before praying while in the air are:

> 1. Prayer times are based on the time zone that the plane is in at the time when the prayer is required, not by the departure or arrival time zones.

2. One must determine the direction of the Ka'bah (the *qibla*) on board the airplane, even if it means asking a flight attendant or (before takeoff) the pilot if necessary. If you cannot verify the proper direction, Muslim scholars say that you can pray in the direction that you think is most likely the *qibla*. (Muslims traveling from North America to the Middle East can pray toward the front of the airplane, for the plane is heading northeast, which is the direction of the Ka'bah from North America. On their way back to North America, they can pray toward the back of the plane).

3. One must seek an area in the airplane to perform prayers in full regular movements, such as the kitchen of the plane, aisle, or an open space in first class or business class, if available. If for some reason you are not able to perform the prayer in its proper manner, then you can pray while seated (if you cannot stand up), nodding slightly for bowing (*ruku*) and placing your forehead on the tray table in front of you to substitute for prostration (*sajdah*).[265]

4. Make sure you have *wudhu* before starting your prayer.

5. Since Islam offers alternatives to praying in full ordinary manner under extenuating circumstances, you cannot defer

---

[265] Some scholars state that if one cannot prostrate properly, then one should also nod his head for prostration instead of placing his forehead on the tray table. In this case, one will nod his head slightly more than the nodding for bowing. Hence, there will be three nods, one for bowing and two for prostration.

your prayers until you arrive at your destination if the time for prayers will expire by the time you arrive there.

6. One must perform the prayers in accordance with the laws that govern prayers while traveling (see Question 100).

113. When making prayers (Salat) at home, can a woman pray behind her husband in congregation?

The leader of the congregational prayer (*Imam al-Jama'at*) must acquire the quality of justice, meaning that one should be actively committed to the religion. Justice is interpreted as someone who does not commit big sins and does not insist on committing the minor sins. If, in one's judgment, a husband has acquired this quality, then one can pray behind him; otherwise one cannot.

114. If a person does not understand the Arabic of the prayers, then what should they do?

Learning the entire Arabic language is not mandatory in Islam; however, learning the Arabic required for prayers is mandatory because the prayers must be recited in Arabic. The words of the prayer should also be comprehended.

A Muslim who just converted to Islam and does not understand or speak Arabic is exempted from this condition as long as he or she is engaged in an active learning process, meaning that he or she is not required to comprehend the Arabic words while making an effort to better understand them. A new convert must still perform the daily prayers with as much Arabic as possible. However, according to some scholars, there are parts of the prayer that a Muslim does not have to read in Arabic, such as the *qunoot*, which is the recommended supplication after the short chapter in the second unit. Other recommended supplications which are recited in the prayer, whether they are in the *qunoot*, bowing, or prostration (*sujood*) are also not required to be recited in Arabic according to some scholars.

115. Can a Muslim pray anywhere and on anything?

As for the first part of the question, a Muslim can pray anywhere as long as the place is permissible and lawful for you to use, meaning that either you own the place or at least have permission from its rightful owner to use it if it is privately owned. If it is known for sure that the owner gives consent for you to use that place, then there is no need to obtain explicit permission. In public places, such as parks, one does not need to obtain permission. Praying on usurped land or a place where you do not have permission to pray will invalidate the prayer.

A Muslim can pray on anything as long as it does not transmit impurity, meaning the place cannot be impure and wet or moist at the same time. So if the ground on which you are standing is impure but dry, then the prayer will be valid, although it is highly recommended to purify it. With respect to choosing the place where the forehead will touch the ground, however, one must observe the following two conditions:

1. It should be totally pure, even if it is dry.

2. It should be part of the earth or that which grows from the earth, provided that it is not worn or eaten.

Acceptable materials to put one's forehead upon include: wood, grass, paper, tree leaves, rocks, tile (if not made of plastic or covered with paint or glassy material), dirt, sand, and soil.

According to many narrations, both from the books of the Sunni and Shia, when Prophet Muhammad (ṣ) prayed in his mosque (*masjid*), he used to pray on pure soil or natural dirt that covered the ground. When praying at home, he used to pray on a *khomira*, a piece of cloth containing some dirt. The Prophet of Islam (ṣ) said: "Earth has been made for me pure and a place for prostration."[266]

We understand from this narration that only earth or a part of it can be suitable for prostration. The Imams of Ahlul Bayt teach us that it is not sufficient to place our foreheads on objects that are worn or edible, so items such as wool, cotton, silk, and common carpets are not permissible to prostrate on.

One can surmise that the rationale behind praying on earth and what grows out of it (but is not edible or worn) is that it is a daily reminder of our final fate, when we all will return to the earth after death and become part of its soil. Moreover, praying on earth trains us to become humble and down to earth. Clothes and food are considered valuable. God wants us to prostrate on objects that we do not deem valuable so that we can achieve a greater level of humbleness and rid ourselves of arrogance.

---

[266] *Sahih al-Bukhari*, vol. 1, p. 113 and *Bihar al-Anwar*, vol. 77, p. 147

116. Can one's nose touch the floor during prostration (*sujood*)?

There are seven parts of our body that must touch the floor during prostration: the forehead, the two palms, the two knees, and the two big toes. For women, it is recommended to put their elbows on the ground during prostration, while for men it is better that they keep them raised off of the ground. It is also recommended that the tip of the nose touch the ground during prostration, preferably upon something similar to that which was used for the forehead.

117. How should one go about making up many missed prayers?

Missed prayers do not have to be made up in the order that they were missed, except for two prayers. The noon (*dhuhr*) prayer must always be performed before the afternoon (*asr*) prayer of the same day; and the evening (*maghrib*) prayer must always be performed before the night (*isha*) prayer of the same day. In other words, if a person is making up for an entire day of missed prayers, then one should perform the evening and night prayers before or after the morning prayer and then follow with the noon and afternoon prayers.

Assume you missed ten days of prayer. You have several ways of making them up. The easiest and least confusing way is this:

Fajr → *Dhuhr* → *Asr* → *Maghrib* → *Isha*

You would repeat this sequence ten times and then you have made up your missed prayers.

You may also make up all of the *Fajr* prayers by praying ten of them, then pray *Dhuhr* & *Asr* ten times, then pray *Maghrib* & *Isha* ten times.

You may also make up the *Dhuhr* & *Asr* prayers first, then move on to the *Fajr* prayer, then move on to the *Maghrib* & *Isha* prayers. Just make sure you do not pray *Dhuhr* ten times then pray *Asr* ten times, because you cannot separate between the *Dhuhr* and *Asr* prayers. Each *Dhuhr* prayer must be followed by an *Asr* prayer, so you must pray *Dhuhr* then *Asr*, and you repeat this set ten times. The same applies to the *Maghrib* and *Isha* prayers as well.

If the prayers missed were during travel, and in that journey, one was obligated to perform the prayers in the shortened format, then instead of praying four units for the noon, afternoon, and night prayers, one must pray two units for each of them missed. A narration from Prophet Muhammad (ṣ) says that if someone has missed a prayer, then he shall perform it as it was missed.[267] In other words, pray a "traveling" prayer for the missed "traveling" prayers, and pray a "full" prayer for the missed "full" prayers.

The timing for making up missed prayers is irrelevant; meaning that it does not have to be the time for the morning prayer in order to make up a missed morning prayer; nor does it have to be time for noon prayer in order to make up a missed noon prayer. One can make up missed prayers at any time of the day. However, one should not delay making up the missed prayers. As soon as you get a chance, make them up, for you never know how long you will live and whether you will have the chance to make them up in the future or not. Try to fulfill your obligations as soon as possible.

---

[267] *Awali al-Li'ali*, by al-Ahsa'i, vol. 2, p. 54

118. When can someone hire another person to perform the prayers he or she has missed?

If a living person has missed any mandatory prayers, then he or she alone must make them up. There are no alternatives. Modifications may be arranged for those who cannot do the prayer in full form (e.g., sitting throughout the prayer as opposed to standing, bowing, and prostrating according to one's ability). However, if due to negligence, a person dies before making up the missed prayers, then the oldest son must make up his father's missed prayers.[268]

A person who has missed prayers may stipulate in his or her will to have them made up after he or she dies from one-third of the money or wealth that he or she leaves behind. Using money from this one third, someone can be hired to make up missed prayers on behalf of the deceased. However, it must be kept in mind that someone else performing the missed prayers does not rule out the possibility of certain reckoning in the hereafter for the deceased person (for not fulfilling his or her own responsibilities). Hence, we should not think that if we neglect our prayers we will be off the hook if we simply have someone make them up for us after we die. Neglecting the prayers is a grave sin.

119. Does a convert have to make up the prayers for all the years that he or she missed before becoming a Muslim?

A convert does not have to make up any of the prayers he or she "missed" prior to converting to Islam. In fact, a narration from

---

[268] According to Ayatollah Sistani this applies only if the son was mature when the father died.

Prophet Muhammad (ṣ) says: "Islam washes off all of the prior sins."[269] Therefore, a convert does not need to make up for the missed prayers, or for any of the other obligations such as fasting (*sawm*), the 20 percent wealth tax (*khums*), or giving alms for the poor (*zakat*). This might be viewed as a "credit" for those who convert to Islam. God wants to make it easier on converts and encourage everyone to embrace the religion of truth.

A convert must make up only those prayers that he or she missed after becoming a Muslim.

120. Is it necessary to make up prayers performed incorrectly, if at the time they were thought to have been prayed correctly?

Each prayer (*salat*) consists of two main parts: pillars or indispensable parts (*arkan*) and normal parts (*ajza'a*). The pillars are:

1. Intention (*niyyat*);

2. Acknowledging God's greatness (*takbeer*);

3. Standing after *takbeer* and before bowing (*ruku*);

4. Bowing (*ruku*);

5. The two prostrations (*sujood*).

Any other component of the prayer is a normal part. Therefore it should be noted in what part of the prayer the mistakes were made.

---

[269] *Bihar al-Anwar*, vol. 6, p. 23

If the errors compromised one of the pillars, then one will need to make up those prayers. But if the errors compromised the normal parts, then one should correct them in the future, but it is not necessary to make up those prayers.

For example, if one completely skips a pillar such as the declaration of God's greatness or the bowing, then the prayer will be void and one needs to make it up. However, if a person performs one of the parts incorrectly, such as making a mistake in the recitation (*dhikr*), then the prayer is still good, but one must try to correct this in future prayers.

121. How can a person pray for a loved one who has passed away?

There are many narrations from Prophet Muhammad (ṣ) and our Imams that state it is highly recommended for the living members of a family to remember their deceased ones by performing good deeds on their behalf.

One way is to give the reward of a prayer to the deceased. For example, one prays a recommended prayer and then after finishing the prayer offers the reward to a beloved deceased. One may simply say: "O God, I gift the reward of this prayer to so and so." According to some traditions, God will then bestow the reward for this particular prayer on both the deceased and the individual performing the prayer.

While a two-unit prayer may seem insignificant to us, it is incredibly valuable and beneficial to our deceased. When the Prophet once passed by a family who was grieving the death of their beloved one, he said, "Two quick units of prayer which you may belittle are better for your deceased than the entire world."[270]

One can also pray for the deceased loved ones, particularly one's parents, by reciting any supplication and gifting it to them. However, it is recommended to offer supplications that are mentioned in the main supplication books and the Qur'an (those that mention parents, for example).

Note that when we pray for a deceased loved one, we are not praying directly to them. Rather, the prayer is to God to shower mercy upon that deceased person. Muslims pray only to God and no other being—alive or dead—is entitled to be worshipped.

122. Can Muslims pay someone to make up all of the prayers that their deceased parents missed, or does the family have to perform it themselves?

If a father dies without making up his missed prayers, then his oldest son must perform those prayers.[271] The oldest son can choose to do them himself or pay someone else to make them up.

If a man does not have any sons or his oldest child is not a male, then it is not mandatory on the other children to make up for their father's missed prayers. However, it remains highly recommended for his close relatives, including his daughters, to make up the missed prayers for the father or to at least hire someone else to perform them.

---

[270] *Mizan al-Hikma*, vol. 3, p. 2480

[271] According to Ayatollah Sistani, this applies only if the son was mature when the father died.

If a mother dies without making up her missed prayers, then although it is not mandatory on her eldest son to make them up, it is highly recommended for her sons and daughters to make them up for her.

Many narrations urge us to offer good deeds on behalf of our parents after they pass away. One narration warns us that even if we treated our parents well when they were alive, but did not offer good deeds on their behalf once they passed away, then God will consider us undutiful to our parents and as if we mistreated them. [272] Therefore, amongst the best deeds that we can offer on their behalf is to make up their missed prayers.

123. Is the lecture (*khutba*) during Friday prayer (*Salat al-Jumu'ah*) counted as two units (*rak'at*)?

Provided that there are at least two sermons, the lecture would be counted as taking the place of the two rak'at.

Normally the first and second sermons take the place of the first and second units of prayer, respectively; then the congregational formal prayer of Friday (*Salat al-Jumu'ah*) begins, which counts for the remaining two units. In this case, the lecture and the congregational Friday prayer take the place of the noon (*dhuhr*) prayers, and it is not necessary to pray the noon prayer.

However, some scholars say that as a precaution, a person should perform the noon prayer as well during the occultation of the twelfth Imam (a), which is why you observe many people praying four units between the Friday prayer and the afternoon (*asr*) prayer. Since the two sermons replace two units of prayer,

---

[272] *Al-Kafi*, vol. 2, p. 163, hadith no. 21

scholars believe that it is highly recommended for individuals attending the Friday prayer to listen to them.

124. Is it recommended to perform the noon (*dhuhr*) prayer after Friday prayer (*Salat al-Jumu'ah*) in congregation?

According to Shia Muslim scholars, during the time of the occultation of the twelfth Imam (a), the Friday is a recommended (*mustahab*) prayer, and thus not obligatory to recite. Certain requirements must be met to perform the Friday prayer properly, and if they are all met and an individual chooses to perform it, then there is no need to pray the noon (*dhuhr*) prayer for that day. The requirements for Friday prayer are:

1. A righteous Imam must lead the prayer.

2. There should be a minimum of five adults attending the prayer, including the Imam.

3. There should be a minimum of three miles separating two Friday prayers held in one town. In large communities, there may indeed be more than one Friday prayer going on at the same time within the prescribed radius of three miles. In this case, only the first Friday prayer that is performed is valid. All of the other Friday prayers within three miles are invalid. The noon prayer then becomes mandatory on those who did not pray the Friday prayer with the first congregation. As a precaution, since it is often difficult to ascertain which center performed the Friday prayer first, many Muslims also perform the noon prayer, even though their Friday prayer may have been valid. The intention is to pray the noon prayer

bima fil dhimma, which basically means that one is praying it in case it is obligatory.

A minority of jurists believes that holding only the Friday prayer during the occultation of the twelfth Imam (a) (which has been the case since the year 260 AH or 874 AD) is not sufficient. These scholars hold to the belief that if the Friday prayer is held, then it is still a mandatory precaution to recite the noon prayer afterwards. However, all scholars believe that at the time of the Imam's return, it becomes mandatory for all Muslim men to attend the Friday prayers except those who are sick or traveling.

125. What is the best way to remember someone in your prayers or supplications (*du'a*)?

The best way someone can include other people in his prayers or supplications (*du'a*) is by praying for them during mandatory or recommended prayers. For instance, the best way to pray for a friend or a brother in faith is to include him in the supplication of the midnight prayer in which you do *istighfar* (ask for God's forgiveness) for forty believers by name. It is even better if such prayers are made while visiting holy shrines and sites such as the holy mosques in Mecca and Medina and the splendid shrines of our revered Imams.

It has been narrated by Prophet Muhammad (ṣ) that God accepts the supplication of a Muslim for his brothers and sisters in faith before He accepts a supplication of the person praying. Also, it has been narrated that one of the best places to conduct a supplication which God will most likely accept is under the dome of Imam al-Husayn's (a) shrine in Karbala, Iraq. Prophet

Muhammad (ṣ) said that God has honored Imam al-Husayn (a) by giving him three virtues:

1. Accepting prayers offered under his dome;

2. Healing from illness in the soil of the immediate vicinity of his burial site; and

3. A lineage of nine Imams (a) from his offspring, beginning with his son Imam Ali Zain al-Abideen (a).[273]

126. Where can one find the texts for the *du'as* that are commonly used in *qunoot* (voluntary *supplication*)?

One can find these du'as in supplication books, such as the English publication "*Call on Me I Answer You.*" These supplications are taken from the Qur'an and the hadith of the Prophet and his immaculate family.

The Qur'an also contains some beautiful supplications that are recommended for recitation during the supplications of prayer. For instance, the last verse in chapter 2 of the Qur'an (*Al-Baqara*) contains a beautiful supplication that many scholars recite in their own prayers:

Our Lord! do not punish us if we forget or make a mistake; Our Lord! do not lay on us a burden as You did lay on those before us, Our Lord do not impose upon us that which we do not have the strength to bear; and pardon us and grant us protection and have mercy on us, You are our Patron, so help us against the unbelieving people.[274]

---

[273] *Wasa'el al-Shia*, vol. 14, p. 423
[274] *Noble Qur'an*, Suratul Baqarah (2), verse 286

Other verses from the Qur'an recited in the supplications of the prayer include:

> And there are some among them who say: Our Lord! Grant us good in this world and good in the hereafter, and save us from the chastisement of the fire.[275]

> Our Lord, pour down upon us patience, and make our steps firm and assist us against the unbelieving people.[276]

However, our scholars believe that the best du'a for recitation in the Qunoot is what is known as "Words of Ease" (*Kalimat al-Faraj*).[277]

> There is no god except God the Forbearing, the Generous; there is no god except God the Highest, the Magnificent. Glory be to God the Lord of the seven heavens and Lord of the seven earths and of all that is in them, and all that is between them, and all that is beneath them and He is the Lord of the great throne. Peace of God be upon all of the Messengers and Praise is for God, Lord of the Worlds.[278]

127. When reciting the Qur'an, what verses require prostration?

There are many *ayaat* (verses) in the Qur'an where it is recommended for a Muslim to prostrate after listening to them,

---

[275] *Noble Qur'an*, Suratul Baqarah (2), verse 201

[276] *Noble Qur'an*, Suratul Baqarah (2), verse 250

[277] This supplication is called the "Words of Ease" because it offers great comfort and relief if it is recited to a dying person.

[278] *Man La Yahtharahul Faqeeh*, vol. 1, p. 490, hadith no. 1409

but it is mandatory to go into a state of prostration for only four verses:

1. Chapter 32, The Prostration (*Al Sajda*), verse 15
2. Chapter 41, Expounded (*Fussilat*), verse 38
3. Chapter 53, The Star (*Al Najm*), verse 62
4. Chapter 96, The Clot (*Al Alaq*), verse 19

While the prostration is mandatory, it is not necessary to prostrate in the direction of Mecca or to make ablution; nor is it mandatory to recite anything while prostrating. It is permissible to prostrate on any object, such as wool or cotton. Prostration for these verses is mandatory not only for the orator or reader but also for the listener as well according to many Jurists. So listening to them while driving a car, for example, would require one to stop and prostrate.

128. When does water become impure (*najis*)?

Scholars divide water into two types: plain water and diluted water. Examples of diluted water are grape water, rose water, orange juice, and soft drinks. Diluted water will become impure (*najis*) any time a drop or more of impurity falls into it, such as urine, blood, or semen. However, plain water does not become impure that easily.

Scholars have further divided plain water into two types: immunized and non-immunized. Immunized water is any quantity of 384 liters (approximately 101 gallons) or more. Hence, oceans, rivers, lakes, swimming pools, ponds, and rain are all deemed to be immunized water. Such water does not become impure unless the color, smell, or taste changes unfavorably when coming into contact with an impurity. For example, if a drop of blood falls in a swimming pool that has more than 384 liters of water, then that water is not considered impure. If enough blood falls into the pool such that the color, smell, or taste of the pool water changes to that of blood, then the water will become impure.

On the other hand, non-immunized water (any quantity less than 384 liters) will become impure even if a drop of impurity falls into it. The watering can people use in the bathroom can be contaminated in such a way.

An exception for non-immunized water is a sink or bathtub with a faucet. With an inflow of fresh water, a standard bathtub full of water can be purified if it becomes contaminated; but isolated water in a tub that is not connected to a faucet will remain impure.

Water with chemicals such as chlorine is still considered plain water, and the rules of plain water apply to it, not the rules of diluted water.

129. Is it true that if one does not wash one's private parts after using the bathroom, the angels curse that person?

According to some narrations, among the actions that will inflict torture in the grave is neglecting to wash oneself after using the bathroom.

Islam places great emphasis on cleanliness and hygiene. Human excrement is highly contaminated with germs, microbes, and disease agents. For instance, our kidneys serve to purify our blood by excreting all of the waste and toxic elements that we consume throughout the day. Therefore, every drop of urine is filled with contaminated elements.

After using the bathroom, whether after urinating or having a bowel movement, one must clean oneself thoroughly with water before engaging in any prayer (*salat*). If this is not done, then the prayer will be invalid. In addition, if there are traces of urine or feces on the body or clothes, one's prayer will also be invalid. Therefore, since the correctness or validity of the prayer is partially based on external cleanliness, it is crucial that a Muslim rinses after using the bathroom.

130. How is one supposed to wash oneself after using the bathroom? If one does not have a water can, then can one put water in one's hand from the sink and wash three times?

After using the bathroom, a person must clean one's private parts. After urinating, a man needs to wash the tip of the penis with some water. If one uses running water from a hose, then washing oneself one time will be sufficient to purify the body from any impurity. If one uses a container or cup, then one must rinse the area two times for it to become pure.

Furthermore, men are highly advised to perform what is called *istibraa* after urinating. Traces or remnants of urine usually stay in the urethra after urination, and sometimes moisture is discharged from the penis but it is not clear whether that moisture is urine or something else (such as perspiration). In this case, one must treat this moisture as if it is urine, which means that one's *wudhu* becomes invalid and one's clothing is considered impure. Since this presents a difficulty to most men (as they have to redo their wudhu and change their clothing that came in contact with that moisture every time they notice unknown moisture being discharged), they can avoid this difficulty by clearing the urethra of any urine through the process of *istibraa,* which involves pressing the penis three times to clear it of urine. Once this is done, any unknown moisture that is discharged will be considered pure. [279]

A woman must wash her entire vaginal area as it is often contaminated by urine when urinating. This will be sufficient to become pure (*tahir*).

After a bowel movement, a person must clean the anus with water in such a way that no traces of stool are left. It does not matter where the water comes from, whether it is from a water can or a hose, though using a hose is preferable and is more effective. In an emergency where water cannot be found, then a minimum of three pieces of cloth or tissue paper would be sufficient to clean the area as long as traces of stool are totally removed. If the traces are not removed by the third usage, then as many pieces of tissue paper as needed to remove them is required.

131. If one passes gas, what kind of ablution (*wudhu*) is necessary?

There are certain things that make ablution (*wudhu*) invalid, such as urinating, emptying the bowel, sleeping, passing out (fainting), and passing gas. For passing gas, the only obligation required is to make ablution to be in a state of purity again. Ablution is done in

---

[279] For details on how *istibraa* is done, refer to your Marja's book of rulings or ask a scholar.

the same way for everything that negates it. Hence, the ablution done after sleeping is the same as the ablution made after passing gas.

132. Is ablution (*wudhu*) required before touching or reciting the Qur'an? What about when a woman is in her menstrual cycle?

Reading the Qur'an at any time does not require ablution (*wudhu*), but without it, a Muslim must not touch the writing of the Qur'an in Arabic (translations are exempt from this, but one is still not permitted to touch the name of God in any language or the names of the Prophet and his noble family). One may touch only the outer cover and the margins of the pages if one is not in a state of ablution. Obviously, it is more respectful to recite the Qur'an while one is in a state of purity and having wudhu, and it is also more rewarding.

Women in their monthly cycle can read any chapter or verse of the Qur'an except the following:

1. Chapter 32, The Prostration (*Al Sajdah*)
2. Chapter 41, Expounded (*Fussilat*)
3. Chapter 53, The Star (*Al Najm*)
4. Chapter 96, The Clot (*Al Alaq*)

Women in their monthly cycle cannot read any part of these four chapters because they contain a mandatory prostration equivalent to prayer. Since women are exempt from praying during their monthly cycles, they are prohibited from reciting these four chapters. They can read any other part of the Qur'an provided they do not touch the Arabic script, and they can also recite any other supplication (*du'a*) narrated by our beloved Imams.

133. If someone performs ablution (*wudhu*) and while wet, touches leather whose source is unknown, (i.e., the leather is not known to be permissible), then is the ablution invalid?

The ablution (*wudhu*) remains valid if the source is unknown. If someone touches leather that is unknown or even unlawful, then the area that came into contact with it should be washed, but his or her ablution remains valid.

134. Can Muslims pray while wearing a leather jacket, belt, wallet, or other accessories?

Wearing a leather jacket, belt, or wallet during prayer is not prohibited (*haram*) if the leather is from a permissible (*halal*) source (e.g., cow, sheep, etc.) and the animal was slaughtered according to Islamic law (*sharia*).

If the source is known to be prohibited, either because it was not slaughtered in an Islamic way or it is made from non-halal animals such as tigers, then it is forbidden to wear it during prayer and doing so will invalidate one's prayers. But if the source is unknown, then it is lawful to pray with such accessories.

Some scholars[280] believe that leather items made in non-Muslim countries are still permissible to wear as long as there is a reasonable chance (5 percent or greater) that they are made from permissible leather. This applies to countries with significant Muslim minorities such as France (10 percent Muslim) and Germany (5 percent Muslim). In addition, this applies to non-

---

[280] Ayatollah Sistani.

Muslim countries that are known to import leather from Muslim countries.

135. In what circumstances is a ceremonial shower (ghusl) necessary? What is the correct method for performing that shower?

The ceremonial shower is indicated or becomes mandatory in the following cases:

1. After intercourse or ejaculation (*janaba*).

2. For women, after finishing the monthly menstrual cycle (*haydh*);

3. During irregular, post-menstrual bleeding (*istihadha*);

4. And post-delivery (*nifas*). No more than ten days after delivery, women must take a ceremonial shower. Bleeding after ten days is considered to be irregular bleeding (*istihadha*).

5. After touching a dead body that has lost its natural heat, and prior to its being washed.

6. Whenever one has taken a pledge (*nadhr*) to do it.

Other times when it is recommended to take a ceremonial shower are before putting on *ihram* for *hajj* or *umrah* (purified clothing for the greater or lesser pilgrimage to Mecca), Friday mornings before noon-time, and before visiting the tomb of Prophet Muhammad (ṣ) or an infallible Imam.

There are other recommended ceremonial showers on the night of important Islamic events, such as Eid al-Fitr, Eid al-Adha, Eid al-Ghadeer, the 15th of Sha'ban (the birth of Imam al-Mahdi (a)), the Nights of Power (*Laylatul Qadr*), and amongst others, the 27th of Rajab (the day when the first verses of the Qur'an were revealed to Prophet Muhammad (ṣ)).

All ceremonial showers are done by one of two methods: either all at once, by submerging the entire body, including the head, totally under water (such as in a swimming pool); or more gradually by washing the head and neck first, then the right side of the body, and then the left side of the body. In both methods, any impurities such as semen, urine, or blood should be removed prior to conducting the *ghusl*. The *ghusl* must be taken with plain water, and the water must be pure and lawful, meaning that it is either lawfully owned or one has permission from its owner to use it.

136. Why do Muslims still rely on physical sighting of the moon to signal a new month rather than on scientific calculations which can give the exact time for the birth of a new moon?

Most scholars state that we cannot rely on scientific calculations for the sighting of the moon because our traditions have stated that "when you see the moon, then start fasting" or "end your fasting."[281] So the keywords are "if you *see*," and with scientific calculations, personal sight is not involved, so we cannot rely on them totally.

Moreover, Prophet Muhammad (ṣ) could have asked Angel Gabriel to tell him exactly when the moon would appear instead of going out to look for it himself. Angel Gabriel could have given him the precise answer by asking God. But the Prophet never did that, showing us that we too must *see* the moon. Therefore, most scholars state that sighting the moon cannot be based only on scientific calculations.

---

[281] *Wasa'el al-Shia*, vol. 10, p. 256. Alulbayt ed.

However, some scholars believe that if scientific calculations strongly indicate that the moon will be large enough to be sighted by the naked eye, then we can rely on them. In other words, we need to know that the moon could be sighted, and if that is the case, then scientific calculations can be accepted according to these scholars.

It is important to address a common misconception here. Some people believe that those scholars who stipulate that the moon must be seen by the naked eye do not believe in science or they do not find science reliable. This is not the case. Their ruling has nothing to do with their attitude towards science. If something is scientifically proven, none of our scholars will hesitate in accepting it. Their ruling is simply based on their understanding of the abovementioned narration, which instructs us to see the moon, and therefore their understanding is that it must be seen by the naked eye.

137. Does one have to pay a financial penalty for days of fasting missed during the Month of Ramadhan, even if one is making them up?

The answer depends on the reason for not fasting during the Month of Ramadhan. Legitimate reasons include being ill, traveling, or pregnancy and breast-feeding which can be adversely affected by fasting. In the case of being ill or traveling, all that needs to be done is to make up the fasting prior to the next Ramadan. In case of pregnancy or breast-feeding, in addition to making up each day of missed fasting, a fidya (which is explained below) for each day must also be paid.

However, if the reason was not legitimate, then in addition to making up the fasting, one day for each day missed, one must also pay a penalty called *kaffara*. The penalty can be either of the following:

1. Feed sixty poor people for each day of fasting missed. The minimum to be paid is the value of 750 grams of wheat per day.
2. Fast sixty consecutive days for *each* day of fasting missed. The missed day of fasting itself must also be made up and added to the penalty to be paid.

Anyone who has missed any days of fasting for legitimate reasons but did not make them up before the next Ramadhan, he or she must make up each day and also pay a penalty called a *fidya*, which is feeding one person the equivalent of 750 grams of wheat for each day not made up before the next Ramadhan. The *fidya* must also be paid by those who cannot fast due to chronic medical conditions. Fasting is not obligatory upon them and they do not need to make up their fast, but they must pay the *fidya* for each day (so they pay the equivalent of feeding thirty poor people every year).

138. According to Ayatollah Sistani, allowing thick dust to reach the throat invalidates the fast. Is household dust, commonly found on cabinets, closets, furniture, and shelves, considered being thick dust?

Household dust is not considered to be thick dust. Thick dust is like that created by smoking or by a sandstorm.

139. Is it prohibited (*haram*) to fast on the day of Ashura (10th of the month of Muharram)?

It is not prohibited (*haram*) to fast on the day of Ashura. However, on the tenth day of Muharram, the day of Ashura, it is highly not recommended (*makrooh*) to fast the entire day.

It is recommended that Muslims refrain from eating and drinking on that day from dawn until the hour after noon, which corresponds to the time of day in which Imam al-Husayn (a) was martyred. But to make the intention of fasting from dawn to sunset is not recommended.

Once the Umayyad Dynasty killed Imam al-Husayn (a), they declared Ashura as a day of joy and celebration, and thus they encouraged people to fast on that day. In the Islamic tradition, fasting is often recommended on important Islamic occasions that mark a celebration or a jovial event. The Umayyad Dynasty forged false narrations stating that Prophet Muhammad (ṣ) used to fast on Ashura. Hence, we are to commemorate the day of Ashura as an exceptional day of mourning, and we should refrain from upholding the false legacy of the Umayyad Dynasty.

140. What is the penalty (kaffara) for breaking an oath with God?

The penalty for breaking an oath with God is to feed ten poor people.

The Twelve Shia Imams

1. Ali ibn Abi Talib (A.D. 600–661): Imam Ali's(a) father, Abu Talib (a), also raised Prophet Muhammad (ṣ), who served as a father figure while Imam Ali (a), his cousin, was growing up. Imam Ali (a) was the first male to come into Islam and went on to marry Prophet Muhammad's (ṣ) daughter Fatima (a). Imam Ali (a) was the father of Shia Islam and the rightful successor to the Prophet, who was his only earthly superior in the annals of Islamic spirituality and history. Imam Ali (a) is buried in Najaf, Iraq.

2. Hasan ibn Ali (A.D. 625–669): Imam Ali's (a) eldest son by Fatima (a), Imam Hasan (a), is known for his battles with Mu'awiyah, a ruler from the Umayyad clan who claimed the caliphate for himself from Damascus. Imam Hasan (a) reached a peace agreement with him in 668 that ceded the caliphate to Mu'awiyah but required that a council of Muslim delegates select the next caliph. The Shia believe that Mu'awiyah poisoned Imam Hasan (a) soon after and he is buried in Medina, Saudi Arabia.

3. Husayn ibn Ali (A.D. 626–680): The charismatic Imam Husayn (a), brother of Imam Hasan (a), formalized a Shia identity of justice through sacrifice at the Battle of Karbala. Greatly outnumbered by armies from the illegitimate empire that demanded his allegiance, Imam Husayn (a) accepted their vengeance upon him, and the devout believers commemorate his martyrdom annually during the Ashura period, mindful that the evil carried out against him still exists. Imam Husayn (a) is buried in Karbala, Iraq.

4. Ali Zain al-Abideen (A.D. 658–713): Imam Ali Zain al-Abideen (a) escaped death at Karbala because he was ill during the battle. He became known as an esteemed scholar and mourned the slaughter of his family for a lifetime. The son of Imam Husayn (a) and the daughter of the last Sassanid (Persian) emperor, he published a collection of supplications called *Psalms of Islam*, regarded among the Shia as the third most sacred Islamic text, after the Qur'an and Imam Ali's (a) *Peak of Eloquence*. Imam Zain al-Abideen (a) is buried in Medina, Saudi Arabia.

5. Muhammad al-Baqir (A.D. 676–732): Imam Muhammad al-Baqir (a) was the first Imam to descend from Prophet Muhammad (ṣ) through both his maternal and paternal lines. Many gravitated to him for his high scholarship and caring demeanor. After the tragedy of Karbala, he shed new light on the persecution and deeply held beliefs of the Shia. He is buried in Medina, Saudi Arabia.

6. Jafar al-Sadiq (A.D. 702–765): Imam Jafar al-Sadiq (a) is famous as the founder of the Jafari school of thought, the primary Shia interpretation of Islamic law. The four major Sunni schools are Hanbali, Hanafi, Maliki, and Shafei, all named after their respective founders. Imam Jafar al-Sadiq (a), in fact, taught two of them, his contemporaries Abu Hanifah and Malik ibn Anas. Sunnis and Shia alike recognize his legal brilliance. Imam Jafar al-Sadiq (a) is buried in Medina, Saudi Arabia.

7. Musa al-Kadhim (A.D. 745–799): Imam Musa al-Kadhim (a) spent thirty-five years as the head of the Imamate, more than any of the other first eleven Imams. An offshoot of Shi'ism believe that Imam Musa al-Kadhim's (a) older brother Ismail was the rightful

Imam; they are known as the Ismailis, or Seveners. Ismail died young during his father's imamate. Imam Musa al-Kadhim (a) lived in a time of great conflict and suspicion about the Imams. The Abbasid ruler Harun al-Rashid imprisoned him in Baghdad multiple times, and finally poisoned him in prison. He is buried in Baghdad, Iraq with the ninth Imam, Imam Muhammad al-Jawad (a).

8. Ali al-Redha (A.D. 765–818): Like so many Muslim rulers before him, the Abbasid caliph Ma'mun, son of Harun al-Rashid, feared a revolt of the people under the Imams. To prevent such a fate, Ma'mun forced Imam al-Redha (a) to leave his home in Medina and live under the caliphate in Khorasan, a far eastern Persian province. Ma'mun hoped to gain favor with the Shia by naming Imam al-Redha (a) as his successor, but the Imam did not outlive Ma'mun. He died after being poisoned by Ma'mun while traveling with him near Tus, in Iran. Imam al-Redha (a) is buried in Mashad, Iran.

9. Muhammad al-Jawad (A.D. 810–835): Imam al-Jawad (a) assumed the mantle of the imamate at the age of nine and despite his young age, developed a reputation as a formidable public debater, overcoming the most respected scholars of his day. He married the daughter of the Abbasid caliph Ma'mun, who was overjoyed to have his lineage merged with the family of Prophet Muhammad (ṣ). Imam al-Jawad (a) spent his final years in Baghdad under Ma'mun's successor before being killed by poisoning (as with many of the Imams) at the age twenty-five. He is buried in Baghdad, Iraq, near his grandfather Imam Musa al-Kadhim (a).

10. Ali al-Hadi (A.D. 828–868): Imam Ali al-Hadi (a) is known as a great teacher and source of spiritual wisdom, yet he spent the last half of his life either imprisoned or under house arrest in Samarra, Iraq, which used to be the seat of the caliphate. He is buried in Samarra at al-Askari, the Golden Mosque, near his son, Imam Hasan al-Askari (a). Their shrine was bombed by insurgents in February 2006, which set off waves of sectarian violence throughout Iraq. In June 2007, insurgents destroyed the two minarets, which survived the 2006 attack.

11. Hasan al-Askari (A.D. 846–874): Imam Hasan al-Askari (a) spent his entire life either under house arrest or in prison, under the close watch of a succession of Abbasid caliphs in Samarra and Baghdad. Though his contact with almost all of the Shia was limited, he was able to transmit his knowledge discreetly to some important Shia figures and in turn to a growing Shia population. Imam Hasan al-Askari (a) was martyred at a young age and is buried alongside his father in Samarra, Iraq.

12. Muhammad ibn Hasan (Al-Mahdi) (A.D. 868–): Caliphs of the time knew that the twelfth Imam would be the savior and thus took elaborate precautions to prevent Imam Hasan al-Askari (a) from having a successor. Nevertheless, Imam al-Mahdi (a) was born, undetected by those in power, and he went into occultation at the age of five, upon the death of his father. In exceptional circumstances he maintained contact with the Shia community through his deputies. He is still among us but remains in occultation until God chooses for him to return at the end of time together with Prophet Jesus (a) to launch a campaign of global justice and reform.